Subjects and verbs: 1, 2, 3, 4 to infinity

Copyright © 2015 by Ralph Duncans Jr

Subjects And Verbs: 1, 2, 3, 4 to Infinity
Ralph Duncans Jr

ISBN: 978-0-9961766-0-6

This is a simplified grammar textbook.

For

My children
DeeAnna , Ralph, Toyoki and Haruka

Table of Contents

Acknowledgements 7
Instructions 8
A Sentence 9
Subjects 10
Let's Make Sentences 12
   Form of "be" Verbs 12
Action Verbs 13
   (Present Tense) 13
Let's Make Sentences 14
   (Action Verbs) 14
Adding Tenses to Regular and Irregular Verbs 15
   Regular and irregular verbs 15
Adding Tenses to Regular and Irregular Verbs 16
   Special verbs 16
Regular And Irregular Verbs 17
   Definitions – 1~54 17
Regular And Irregular Verbs 18
   Definitions - 55 ~ 97 18
Regular And Irregular Verbs 19
   Definitions - 98 ~ 158 19
Regular And Irregular Verbs 20
   Definitions - 159 ~ 206 20
Regular And Irregular Verbs 21
   Definitions - 207~ 242 21
Making A Present Tense Sentence 22
Making A Sentence 23
   Form of "be" verbs – "is, are" and "am" 23
Making A Sentence 24
   Action Verbs 24
Making A Sentence 25
   Present continuous tense: + ing 25
The Parts Of A Subject 26
   "The, A," and "An" 26
The Parts Of A Subject 27
   Nouns 27
Remember 28
   Subjects and Verbs 28
Let's Make A Sentence 30
   "A, An" and "The" 30
Let's Make A Sentence 31
   "A" and "An" 31

- Let's Make Sentences 32
  - Subjects and form of BE 32
- Let's Make Sentences 33
  - Subjects and Action Verbs 33
- Let's Make A Sentence 34
  - Subjects, form of BE Verbs and Action Verbs. 34
- Let's Make A Sentence 35
  - Subjects and "am, is" and "are." 35
- Let's Make A Sentence 36
  - Subjects and Acton Verbs 36
- Let's Make A Sentence 37
  - Present Continuous Tense: + ing. 37
- Past Tense: Subjects and Verbs 38
- Past Tense: 39
  - Regular and Irregular Verbs 39
- Future Tense: Subjects and Verbs 40
  - Subject + "will" + "be" or an Action verb = 2, 3, 4 ~ ∞ 40
- Present and Past Perfect Tenses 41
  - Has, have or had + a perfect tense verb 41

Acknowledgements

I thank Aaron Baloney for viewing my writings and sharing his perspectives.

Instructions

This grammar book was designed for simplicity. I chose to use numbers to help children comprehend how subjects and verbs are matched. I simply replaced singular and plural with their numerical values. Singular's numerical value is one. Plural's numerical value is 2, 3, 4 ~ infinity. All tests are open notes. The students just have to write the words' corresponding numbers below the words and circle the like numbers, then the correct answer. The last set of tests will require the use of a dictionary. You will need a dictionary that has conjugations in it. The last set of test switches from numerals to singular or plural. The purpose of this text is comprehension. Help students when needed. Give credit for the problems students do themselves. This book will help anyone person of any age to comprehend how subjects and verbs are matched.

If you have any questions contact me at my1english1@gmail.com

A Sentence

s + v = a sentence

=

Now   **Present Tense**

If the number (#) of subjects (s) equals to (=) the number (#) of verbs (v), then the subject (s) plus (+) the verb (v) is (=) a sentence.

If # of s = # of v, then s + v = a sentence

1. <u>Subjects-(s)</u>:

    a. Subjects = 1

    b. Subjects = 2, 3, 4 ~ ∞

2. <u>Verbs-(v)</u>:

    a. **<u>Form of "be" verbs:</u>**

        A. Form of "be" verbs = 1

        B. Form of "be" verbs = 2, 3, 4 ~ ∞

    b. **<u>Action verbs:</u>**

        A. Action verbs = 1

        B. Action verbs = 2, 3, 4 ~ ∞

Subjects
The subject agrees with the verb.
(Present Tense)

a.	b.
Subjects = 1	**Subjects = 2, 3, 4 ~ ∞**

 He = 1

 She = 1

 It = 1

A _____
1 = 1

An _____
ah, eh, ih, oh, uh
1 = 1

*The _____
1 = 1

When there is one person

I = 3 (I, me, myself)

you = 3 (you, you, yourself)

we = 3 (we, us, ourselves)

___

When there are 2, 3, 4 ~ ∞ people

You = 2, 3, 4 ~ ∞ (infinity)
We = 2, 3, 4 ~ ∞
They = 2, 3, 4 ~ ∞

They = $\begin{cases} he & \times\ 2, 3, 4 \sim \infty \\ she & \times\ 2, 3, 4 \sim \infty \\ it & \times\ 2, 3, 4 \sim \infty \end{cases}$

*The _____
2, 3, 4 ~∞ = 2, 3, 4 ~ ∞

*(the = 1, 2, 3, 4 ~ ∞)

Form of "be" Verbs

BE verbs show a condition.

(Present Tense)

A. Form of "be" = 1	B. Form of "be" = 2, 3, 4 ~ ∞
is = 1	are = 2, 3, 4 ~ ∞
He ~~be~~. → He is.	I ~~be~~. → I am. (only I)
She be. → She is.	You be. → You are.
It be. → It is.	We be. → We are.
A ___ be. → A ___ is. 1 = 1 1 = 1	They be. → They are.
An ___ be. → An ___ is. 1 = 1 1 = 1	The __ be. → The __ are. ∞ = ∞ ∞ = ∞
The ___ be. → The ___ is. 1 = 1 1 = 1	

"Be" changes to "am, is" or "are" to agree with the subject in the present tense.

I ~~be~~ happy. → I am happy.

He ~~be~~ sleeping. → He is sleeping.

They ~~be~~ jumping. → They are jumping.

.

11

Let's Make Sentences
Form of "be" Verbs

Circle (◯) the correct verb.

1. You (is), (are).

2. He (is), (are).

3. They (is), (are).

4. We (are), (am).

5. The balls ( ) (am), (are).

6. A car ( ) (are), (is).

7. An orange ( ) (is), (are).

8. The trees ( ) (am), (are).

9. I (am), (is).

10. The cake ( ) (am), (are).

11. She (are), (is).

12. A dog ( ) (am), (is).

13. It (are), (is).

14. It (are), (is).

15. They (are), (is).

16. We (is), (are).

17. The bike ( ) (is), (are).

18. An apple ( ) (am), (is).

19. She (is), (am).

20. You (are), (is).

Action Verbs
Shows an action
(Present Tense)

A.	**B.**
Action verbs = 1	**Action verbs = 2, 3, 4 ~ ∞**
do + es = does = 1	do = 2, 3, 4 ~ ∞
eat + s = eats = 1	eat = 2, 3, 4 ~ ∞
drink + s = drinks = 1	drink = 2, 3, 4 ~ ∞
sleep + s = sleeps = 1	sleep = 2, 3, 4 ~ ∞
jump + s = jumps = 1	jump = 2, 3, 4 ~ ∞
sit + s = sits = 1	sit = 2, 3, 4 ~ ∞
does = sits, runs, eats, talks, climbs, types, drinks, watches, sings, and all other action verbs = 1	do = sit, run, eat, talk, climb, type, drink, watch, sing, and all other action verbs = 2, 3, 4 ~ ∞

Note: Adding an "s" or an "es" changes an action verb = 2, 3, 4 ~ ∞ to an action verb = 1.

(If you are unsure, please check your dictionary and/or a reference book)

Let's Make Sentences
(Action Verbs)

Circle (◯) the correct verb. Use your notes.

1. I (run), (runs).

2. We (eats), (eat).

3. They (drink), (drinks).

4. He (read), (reads).

5. The ball (🎾) (bounce), (bounces).

6. A dog (🐕) (bark), (barks).

7. She (sit), (sits).

8. A pen (✒) (write), (writes).

9. It (✋) (plays), (play).

10. She (sew), (sews).

11. I (sleep), (sleeps).

12. We (jump), (jumps).

13. The bed (🛏) (sleeps), (sleep).

14. The apple (🍎) (eats), (eat).

15. The phones (📱📱) (washes), (wash).

16. They (swim), (swims).

17. He (skates), (skate).

18. You (go), (goes).

19. A book (📖) (reads), (read).

20. A banana (🍌) (stand), (stands).

21. The fish (🐟) (swim), (swims).

22. It (cries), (cry).

23. The boy (🧒) (walks), (walk).

24. She (talks), (talk).

25. A cup (☕) (drink), (drinks).

Adding Tenses to Regular and Irregular Verbs
Regular and irregular verbs

1. <u>Regular verbs:</u> (Some words will need modification.)

    a. Just add the tenses' words or endings to the verb.

    Example: Present tense: walk = 2, 3, 4 ~ ∞

    past tense (+ ed):   present continuous tense (+ ing):

    walk + ed = walked   walk + ing = walking

    Note: The perfect tense and the past tense use the same word.

2. <u>Irregular verbs:</u> (before adding tenses' words or endings)

    a. A letter is dropped.

    Example: come = 2, 3, 4 ~ ∞

    present continuous tense (+ ing): come + ing = com~~e~~ + ing = coming

    b. Nothing changes.

    Example: read = 2, 3, 4 ~ ∞

    past tense (+ ed): read + (ed) = read + ~~ed~~ = read

    Note: read is pronounced "red" in the past tense.

    c. A different word is used.

    Example: be = 1, 2, 3, 4 ~ ∞

    past tense (+ ed): be + (ed) = ~~be + ed~~ → *was* or *were*

    was = 1   were = 2, 3, 4 ~ ∞

    d. A letter changes to another letter.

    Example: come= 2, 3, 4 ~ ∞

    past tense (+ ed): come + (ed) = c(o → a) me+ ~~ed~~ = came

(Note: The perfect tense and the past tense may or may not use the same word.)

(If you are unsure, please check your dictionary and/or a reference book)

Adding Tenses to Regular and Irregular Verbs
Special verbs

3. <u>Special Verbs:</u>

a. The last letter is doubled (consonants only). Doubling the last letter maintains the words' pronunciation.

   Example: Irregular verb: run = 2, 3, 4 ~ ∞

   Present continuous tense (+ ing):

   run + (ing) = ru (n × 2) + ing = ru(nn) + ing = runn + ing = running

   Note:
   Some letters are doubled. Not doubling them will create another word.

   Example: Regular verb: hop = 2, 3, 4 ~ ∞

   Present continuous tense (+ ing): hop = 2, 3, 4 ~ ∞

   hop + ing = hoping

   The present tense form of "hoping" is "hope."

   "Hoping" is a different word with a different meaning.

   Find the words "hop" and "hope" in your dictionary.

   If the last letter is not doubled, a word that may not exist will be formed.

   Example: Irregular verb: run

   Present continuous tense (+ ing): run = 2, 3, 4 ~ ∞

   run + ing = runing

   There is no word "ru • ning" in the English language.

   (If you are unsure, please check your dictionary and/or a reference book)

Regular And Irregular Verbs

Definitions – 1~54

Write the meanings and the past tense (+ ed) forms of these verbs.

1. act	19. build	37. damage
2. add	20. burn	38. decide
3. agree	21. call	39. designs
4. answer	22. camp	40. destroy
5. apply	23. carry	41. discover
6. awake	24. catch	42. discuss
7. bake	25. chain	43. do
8. bat	26. change	44. draw
9. bear	27. check	45. dream
10. begin	28. choose	46. drink
11. believe	29. climb	47. drive
12. bite	30. complain	48. drop
13. block	31. continue	49. earn
14. blow	32. control	50. eat
15. boil	33. cook	51. e-mail
16. borrow	34. cover	52. end
17. break	35. cross	53. enjoy
18. brush	36. cut	54. enter

Regular And Irregular Verbs
Definitions - 55 ~ 97

Write the meanings and the present continuous tense forms (+ing) of these verbs.

55. equal	62. hide	80. leave
56. excuse	63. hope	81. lend
57. expect	64. hug	82. let
58. experience	65. hurry	83. lift
59. explan	66. hurt	84. like
60. express	67. introduce	85. listen
61. feel	68. invent	86. live
62. finish	69. invite	87. look
63. force	70. judge	88. love
64. forget	71. jump	89. make
65. give	72. keep	90. march
55. go	73. kiss	91. marry
56. grow	74. knit	92. master
57. guard	75. knock	93. match
58. guide	76. know	94. matter
59. hang	77. laugh	95. mean
60. have	78. lead	96. meet
61. hear	79. learn	97. mend

Regular And Irregular Verbs

Definitions - 98 ~ 158

Write the meaning and the perfect form of each word.

98. mistake	119. practice	139. record
100. move	120. praise	140. refuse
101. need	121. prepare	141. remain
102. nurse	122. present	142. remember
103. offer	123. press	143. repair
104. open	124. print	144. repeat
105. pack	125. produce	145. report
106. paint	126. promise	146. respect
107. park	127. prove	147. rest
108. part	128. pull	148. result
109. pass	129. punish	149. return
110. pay	130. push	150. ride
111. pin	131. put	151. ring
112. place	132. questions	152. rise
113. plan	133. race	153. roll
114. plant	134. rain	154. root
115. play	135. raise	155. round
116. please	136. reach	156. rule
117. point	137. read	157. run
118. post	138. receive	158. rush

Regular And Irregular Verbs
Definitions - 159 ~ 206

Write the present continuous tense (+ ing) form of these verbs.

159. say	175. shop	191. sound
160. season	176. shout	192. spare
161. seat	177. show	193. spend
162. see	178. shut	194. spot
163. seem	179. sign	195. spread
164. sell	180. signal	196. spring
165. send	181. sing	197. stamp
166. sentence	182. sink	198. stand
167. serve	183. sit	199. start
168. sew	184. skate	200. state
169. shake	185. sleep	201. stay
170. shape	186. slide	202. steal
171. share	187. smell	203. step
172. shine	188. smile	204. stick
173. shock	189. snap	205. stop
174. shoot	190. snow	206. store

Regular And Irregular Verbs
Definitions - 207~ 242

Write the verb = 2, 3, 4 ~ ∞ form of these verbs.

207. stream

208. strike

209. study

210. succeed

211. suppose

212. surprise

213. swim

214. take

215. talk

216. tape

217. taste

218. teach

219. tear

220. test

221. thank

222. think

223. touch

224. train

225. travel

226. treasure

227. trouble

228. turn

229. understand

230. use

231. visit

232. wait

233. walk

234. want

235. wash

236. watch

237. water

238. wear

239. wish

240. work

241. worry

242. write

Making A Present Tense Sentence
s + v = a sentence
\# = \#

1. **Subjects + Form of "be" verbs: am, is, are**

    I am.   He is.   You are.
    s + v   s + v   s + v
    3 = (only I)   1 = 1   ∞ = ∞

    Remember, "am" is only with "I".

2. **Regular and Irregular Action Verbs:**

    a. He + walks = He walks = a sentence
       1 = 1   1 = 1

    Regular Verb: (walk)

    He walks.
    1 = 1

    b. They + sit = They sit = a sentence
       3   = 3   3 = 3

    Irregular Verb: (sit)

    They sit.
    3 = 3

3. **Regular and Irregular Continuous Verbs:**
    A subject + a form of "be" verb (am, is, are) + a present continuous tense verb.

    a. I + am + playing = I am + playing = I am playing = a sentence
          (only I)   (only I)

    Regular verb: (play)   I am playing.

    b. She + is + running = She is + running = She is running = a sentence
       1   = 1   1 = 1

    Irregular verb: (run)   She is running.

    c. They + are + riding = They are + riding = They are riding = a sentence
       2   = 2

    Irregular verb: (ride)   They are riding.

Making A Sentence

Form of "be" verbs – "is, are" and "am".

Write the correct form of "be" in the space.

1. A lion (   ).

2. An envelope (   ).

3. The girls (   ).

4. I (   ).

5. An apple (   ).

6. The triangles (   ).

7. The socks (   ).

8. A car (   ).

9. An octopus (   ).

10. I (   ).

11. A pillow (   ).

12. An eraser (   ).

13. The beds (   ).

14. A bat (   ).

15. I (   ).

16. The [1]jacket (   ).

17. The [2]closet (   ).

18. A [3]rock (   ).

19. An [4]egg (   ).

20. The [5]refrigerator (   ).

[1]jacket = 1

[2]closet = 1

[3]rock = 1

[4]egg = 1

[5]refrigerator = 1

Making A Sentence
Action Verbs

Write the correct present tense form of the verb in the space.

1. The dogs (   ).   eat   (dogs = 2, 3, 4 ~ ∞)
2. A lion (   ).   jump
3. An eye (   ).   read
4. The cars (   ).   drive   (cars = 2, 3, 4 ~ ∞)
5. A cup (   )   write
6. The apple (   ).   draw   (apple = 1)
7. A lake (   ).   crawl
8. An ear (   ).   wash
9. A bike (   ).   sit
10. The glasses (   ).   drink   (glasses = 2, 3, 4 ~ ∞)
11. A shirt (   ).   play
12. An olive (   )   act
13. The world (   ).   clean   (world = 1)
14. A mountain (   ).   try
15. An oyster (   )   do
16. The rocks (   ).   think   (rocks = 2, 3, 4 ~ ∞)
17. A cloud (   ).   study
18. An octopus (   ).   touch
19. The stop sign (   ).   see   (stop sign = 1)
20. A book (   ).   smell

Making A Sentence
Present continuous tense: + ing

Write the correct form of "be" verb and the present continuous tense of the verbs.

1. I _____ _____.   play
2. He _____ _____.   look
3. She _____ _____.   jump
4. We _____ _____.   sleep
5. They _____ _____.   walk
6. The car _____ _____.   drive   (car = 1)
7. An apple _____ _____.   eat
8. It _____ _____.   run
9. I _____ _____.   go
10. We _____ _____.   talk
11. The birds _____ _____.   sing   (birds = 2, 3, 4 ~ ∞)
12. The boat _____ _____.   sail   (boat = 1)
13. A train _____ _____.   come
14. An elbow _____ _____.   bend
15. Cats _____ _____.   cry   (cats = 2, 3, 4 ~∞)
16. Dogs _____ _____.   bark   (dogs = 2, 3, 4 ~ ∞)
17. Shoes _____ _____.   skate (shoes = 2. 3. 4 ~ ∞)
18. The soap _____ _____.   wash   (soap = 1)
19. We _____ _____.   leave
20. A pen _____ _____.   writes

25

The Parts Of A Subject
"The, A," and "An"

1. A _____   An _____
                          ah, eh, ih, oh, uh

Each subject has a special name, only "a," "an" and "the" are discussed.

"A" and "an" are, sometimes, called indefinite articles. Indefinite, basically, means "not special" or "not specific."

"A" and "an" in one word means – general. Nothing special.

"A's" and "an's" value is one (1).

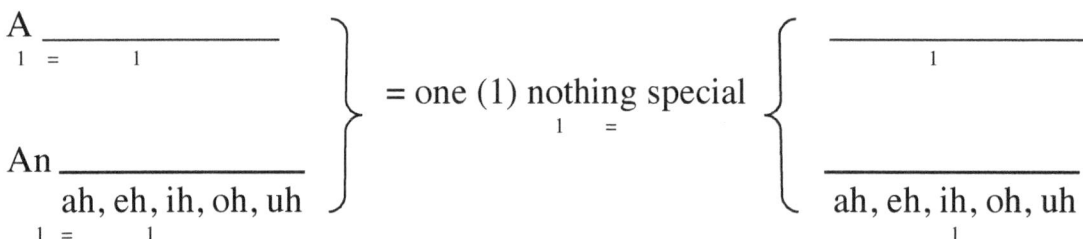

On the line, next to "a" and "an" a noun is used –

      A __noun__   An __noun__

2. The _____

"The" is sometimes called a definite article. "The" in one word means "special" or "specific." "The's" number values are (=) 1, 2, 3 ~ ∞.

The = one, two, three to infinity special or specific

    The _____ = one, two, three to infinity special or specific
_____.
  1, 2, 3 ~ ∞ = 1, 2, 3 ~ ∞

On the line, next to "the" a noun is used.

    The __noun__

Do you know what a noun is?

The Parts Of A Subject
Nouns

A. Singular (1) and plural (2, 3, 4 ~ ∞) nouns.

   1. What is a noun? A noun is a person, a place or a thing.

   2. A noun plus (+) an "s" or an "es" equals (=) 2, 3, 4 ~ ∞.

      Example: ball + s = balls (2. 3. 4 ~ ∞)

        a. balls = 2, 3, 4 ~ ∞   balls = a plural noun

   3. A noun without (-) an "s" or an "es" equals (=) 1

      Example: balls – s = ball (1)

        a. ball = 1   ball = a singular (1) noun

Note: Not all singular (1) nouns add an "s" or an "es" to change the noun to a plural (2, 3, 4 ~ ∞) noun.

Example: sheep

  1. sheep = a singular (1) and a plural (2, 3, 4 ~ ∞) noun

Example: man = a singular (1) noun

  1. men = a plural (2, 3, 4 ~ ∞) noun

    The "a" changes to an "e."

(If you are unsure, please check your dictionary and/or a reference book)

Remember
Subjects and Verbs

1. Subjects:

    a. What are the subjects equal to 1?

    _____   _____   _____

    _____   _____   _____

    b. What are the subjects equal to 2, 3, 4 ~ ∞.

    _____ _____ _____ _____

    c. He + she + it = _____.

    d. I = _____.

2. Verbs:

    a. What are the two types of verbs?

    _____   _____

    b. The form of "be" verb equals to 1 is _____.

    c. The form of "be" verb equals to 2, 3, 4 ~ ∞ is _____.

    d. "Am" is _____.

    e. What is the difference between a plural (2, 3, 4 ~ ∞) action verb and a singular (1) action verb?

    _____

Singular and Plural Nouns

Write the plural form (2, 3, 4 ~ ∞) and the meanings of these nouns.

1. accident	19. joke	37. tiger
2. address	20. judge	38. tongue
3. bat	21. language	39. umbrella
4. bathroom	22. leader	40. university
5. case	23. man	41. view
6. cherry	24. manner	42. volleyball
7. date	25. neck	43. wall
8. doctor	26. noise	44. water
9. examination	27. ocean	45. x-ray
10. eye	28. office	46. year
11. face	29. part	47. yourself
12. family	30. people	48. zero
13. glass	31. queen	49. zoo
14. government	32. question	50. stick
15. harvest	33. reason	51. sky
16. head	34. report	52. plan
17. inch	35. sand	53. morning
18. insect	36. school	54. love

Let's Make A Sentence
"A, An" and "The"

Write the correct form of the noun in the space.

1. A (　　　　) is.　　　　car
2. An (　　　　) goes.　　　orange
3. The (　　　　) are.　　　box
4. A (　　　　) drinks.　　zebras
5. An (　　　　) eats.　　　apples
6. The (　　　　) sews.　　pencil
7. A (　　　　) runs.　　　chain
8. An (　　　　) talks.　　mouths
9. The (　　　　) cook.　　cat
10. A (　　　　) flies.　　hour
11. An (　　　　) climbs.　octopus
12. The (　　　　) roll.　　bikes
13. A (　　　　) jumps.　　rabbit
14. An (　　　　) reads.　　owls
15. The (　　　　) skates.　house
16. A (　　　　) turns.　　rocks
17. An (　　　　) bite.　　dog
18. The (　　　　) plays.　paper

Let's Make A Sentence
"A" and "An"

On the line (_____), write "A" or "An."

1. _____ apple is.

2. _____ book is.

3. _____ egg is.

4. _____ orange eats.

5. _____ boy talks.

6. _____ oval runs.

7. _____ car drives.

8. _____ eagle flies.

9. _____ fish swims.

10. _____ umbrella opens.

11. _____ unicorn stands.

12. _____ octopus eats.

13. _____ computer types.

14. _____ hour goes.

15. _____ house lives.

16. _____ table jumps.

17. _____ anchor drops.

a _____

an _____
a e i o u

Let's Make Sentences
Subjects and form of BE

Circle (○) the correct subject.

1. (He), (They) are.
2. (The ball), (You) are.
3. (We), (A car) is.
4. (The cup), (I) am.
5. (The cakes), (He) is.
6. (A boy), (I) is.
7. (The pen), (They) are.
8. (She), (I) am.
9. (A bed), (We) is.
10. (An apple), (I) is.
11. (He), (The fish) are.
12. (We), (He) is.
13. (The bikes), (She) are.
14. (The phone), (They) are.
15. (Bananas), (I) am.
16. (The tree), (I) is.
17. (Cups), (She) are.
18. (Books), (I) am.
19. (People), (She) are.
20. (The phone), (They) is.
21. (I), (He) am.
22. (She), (I) is.
23. (They), (It) is.
24. (We), (A dog) are.
25. (You), (The fork) is.
26. (An orange), (I) is.
27. (A bed), (She) is.
28. (A chair), (We) are.
29. (He), (You) is.
30. (You), (It) is.

Let's Make Sentences
Subjects and Action Verbs

Circle (◯) the correct subject.

1. (Apples 🍎🍎), (An apple 🍎) eats.
2. (Dogs 🐕🐕), (A dog 🐕) drink.
3. (The tree 🌳), (The trees 🌳🌳) grow.
4. (Bananas 🍌🍌), (The banana 🍌) sit.
5. (The table 🪑), (Tables 🪑🪑) stands.
6. (An orange 🍊), (The oranges 🍊🍊) run.
7. (Cakes 🎂🎂), (A cake 🎂) walk.
8. (The bike 🚲), (Bikes 🚲🚲) rides.
9. (A chair 🪑), (Chairs 🪑🪑), swim.
10. (A toothbrush), (Toothbrushes) shakes.
11. (He), (They) go.
12. (I), (It) comes.
13. (She), (We) write.
14. (They), (He) washes.
15. (He), (I) play.
16. (She), (It) sleeps.
17. (You), (She) do.

Let's Make A Sentence

Subjects, form of BE Verbs and Action Verbs.

Circle (◯) or box (▭) the correct subject with the correct verb.

1. (He), (I) (am), (is).
2. (A pen), (we) (is), (are).
3. (An orange), (You) (are), (is).
4. (The car), (Boys) (is), (are).
5. (We), (I) (sit), (am).
6. (They), (she) (run), (is).
7. (I), (You) (am), (are).
8. (The bike), (We) (are), (goes).
9. (I), (The apple) (eat) (is).
10. (Cups), (It) (are), (jumps).
11. (They), (A fish), (swims) (are).
12. (I), (The books) (am) (sit).
13. (A bed), (You) (are) (talks).
14. (The phone), (We) (rings), (are).
15. (I), (She) (cook), (is).
16. (You), (An apple) (sits), (are).
17. (It), (I) (washes), (am).

Let's Make A Sentence
Subjects and "am, is" and "are."

On the line (_____) write the correct form of BE verb.

1. I (_____).

2. He (_____).

3. She (_____).

4. They (_____)

5. We (_____).

6. You (_____).

7. It (_____).

8. The dog (_____).

9. A car (_____).

10. An orange (_____).

11. The table (_____)

12. Houses (_____).

13. The pillows (_____).

14. Cars (_____).

15. People (_____).

16. A bowl (_____).

17. I (_____).

Let's Make A Sentence
Subjects and Acton Verbs

Write the correct present tense form of the verb in the space (   ).

1. I (   ).   play
2. He (   ).   catch
3. She (   ).   erase
4. They (   ).   read
5. It (   ).   jump
6. We (   ).   skate
7. You (   ).   climb
8. The computer (   ).   bite
9. A boat (   ).   turn
10. Pencils (   ).   roll
11. The shoes (   ).   fly
12. The eraser (   ).   eat
13. A boy (   ).   think
14. People (   ).   go
15. I (   ).   do
16. The chair (   ).   see
17. An orange (   ).   smile
18. It (   ).   have
19. My fingers (   ).   feel
20. You (   ).   know

Let's Make A Sentence
Present Continuous Tense: + ing.

Write the correct form of BE verbs and the present continuous verbs on the line.

1. I _____ _____.   sleep

2. He _____ _____.   fly

3. She _____ _____.   jump

4. A dog _____ _____.   sit

5. An eagle _____ _____.   eat

6. The car _____ _____.   swim

7. It _____ _____.   come

8. They _____ _____.   run

9. We _____ _____.   watching

10. You _____ _____.   dig

11. The trains _____ _____.   write

12. Shoes _____ _____.   roll

13. The water _____ _____.   drip

14. My computer _____ _____.   work

15. Your phone _____ _____.   beep

Past Tense: Subjects and Verbs

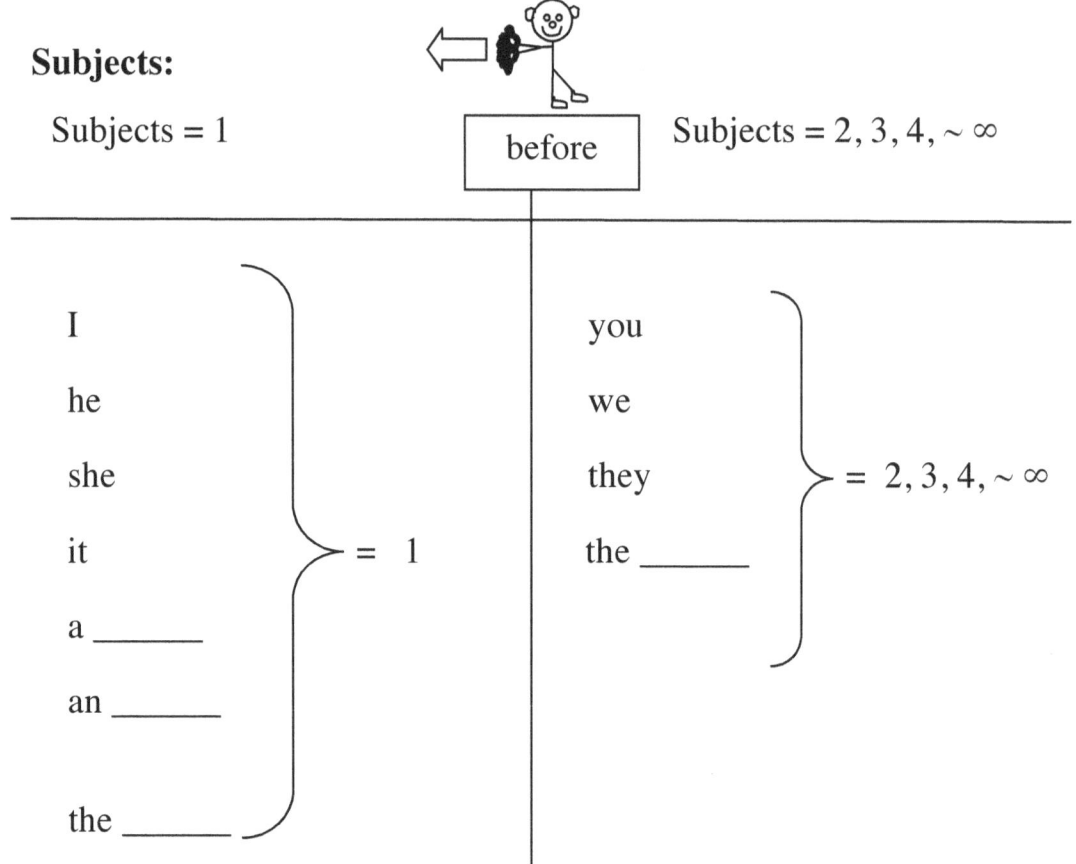

Subjects:

Subjects = 1   before   Subjects = 2, 3, 4, ~ ∞

I, he, she, it, a ___, an ___, the ___ } = 1	you, we, they, the ___ } = 2, 3, 4, ~ ∞

Note: "I" in the present tense is equal to (=) 3. "I" in the past tense is equal to (=) 1.

Form of BE verbs: ("be" is an irregular verb)

Form of "be" verb = 1	Form of "be" verb = 2, 3, 4 ~ ∞
was = 1	were = 2, 3, 4 ~ ∞

Action Verbs: (There are regular and irregular action verbs.)

All past tense action verbs are equal to (=) 1, 2, 3, 4 ~ ∞.

Past Tense:
Regular and Irregular Verbs

Write the past tense form of the verbs on the line.

1. I _____.   love

2. You _____.   are

3. The pen _____.   write

4. An apple _____.   eat

5. A girl _____.   look

6. My shirt _____.   is

7. They _____.   read

8. We _____.   will

9. The paper _____.   float

10. The trees _____.   stand

11. The road _____.   turn

12. She _____.   color

13. He _____.   print

14. The dictionary _____.   hold

15. The stop sign _____.   stop

16. A crayon _____.   color

17. Cars _____.   beep

18. The book _____.   be

39

Future Tense: Subjects and Verbs

Subject + "will" + "be" or an Action verb = 2, 3, 4 ~ ∞.

The subject + "will" +   "be"

a. I will be.

b. He will be.

c. She will be.

d. It will be.

e. A dog will be.

f. An apple will be.

g. The horse will be.

h. You will be.

i. We will be.

j. They will be.

k. The shoes will be.

The subject + "will" + an action verb = 2, 3, 4 ~ ∞

a. I will jump.

b. He will look.

c. She will eat.

d. It will run.

e. A lion will eat.

f. An octopus will move.

g. The chair will sit.

h. You will know.

i. We will understand.

j. They will choose.

k. The children will play.

Note: The word "be" is used in the future tense.

Present and Past Perfect Tenses
Have, has or had + a perfect tense verb

Present Perfect Tense Sentences
   a. He has been to Hawaii.
   b. She has been to Guam.
   c. It has been to Los Angeles.
   d. A dog has sat in here.
   e. An owl has been sitting.
   f. The car has been painted.
   g. I have walked to the store.
   h. You have been to the library.
   i. We have swum at the beach.
   j. They have been to the police.
   k. The oranges have bought in the refrigerator.

Past Perfect Tense Sentences
   a. He had eaten at the beach.
   b. She had been in the building.
   c. It had fallen here.
   d. A lion had eaten the sheep.
   e. An ant had drunk the juice.
   f. The machine had been working.
   g. I had been going.
   h. You had talked to them.
   i. We had been talking.
   j. They had gone home.
   k. The birds had flown south.

www.ingramcontent.com/pod-product-compliance
Lightning Source LLC
Chambersburg PA
CBHW041714290426
44110CB00024B/2831

PLATES 9 & 10.

Plates 9 and 10 exhibit the side and end elevations of a building designed for a warehouse, or mill.

Length of building, 50 feet;
Width of building, 40 feet;
Height of building from the foundation to the top of plates, 36 feet;
Main timbers, 12 inches square;
Door posts, 10 by 12;
Purlin posts, 8 by 10;
Plates and purlin plates, 8 by 8;
Braces, 4 by 6;
Lower joists, 3 by 12;
Upper joists, 3 by 10;
Studding, 2 by 8;
Rafters, 2 by 6.

The posts are framed in sections, one story at a time, on account of the difficulty in procuring long timbers, also for facility in raising the building; for, by this means, each story can be raised separately. It has also been proved by experience, that when the timbers are locked together as represented in the Plate, this mode of building is equally strong as to have the posts in one length. The ends of the joists are sized to a uniform width, and placed upon the timbers, *the crowning side up;* the studs are morticed into the timbers as usual. The roof is framed to a quarter pitch, and the braces to a regular 3 feet run. Plate 3 describes the manner of obtaining the bevels of the rafters and gable-end studding. Plates 7 and 8 show the manner of obtaining the bevels of the purlin posts and braces. Plate 4 gives the method of finding the length of the gable-end studding.

Cripple Studs.

The length of the *cripple studs*, which are to be nailed to the braces, depends upon the run of the braces. The braces in this building, being on a regular run, are all set at an angle of 45 degrees, so the bevel of the cripple studs will be the same; and the rise of the brace being equal to the run, the length of each cripple stud will be equal to the height of the post from the sill to the toe of the brace, added to the distance of the stud from the post. In this building, the height of the brace from the sill to the toe of the brace in the first story, is 8 feet, and the inside of the first stud being 16 inches from the inside of the post, the length of the first cripple stud will be 16 inches longer than the height of the post from the sill to the toe of the brace, or 9 feet, 4 inches; and the length of the next cripple stud will be 16 inches more, or 10 feet 8 inches.

It now remains to determine the bevels and the lengths of those cripple studs in the gable end, which are to come against the purlin posts. Having already (Plate 7) found the bevel at the foot of the purlin post equal to the *upper* end bevel of the *rafters*, it will follow that the bevel of the cripple studs upon the purlin post is equal to the *lower* end bevel of the *rafters*.* The length of the cripple studs standing between the rafter and the purlin posts depends both upon the rise of the roof and the rise of the purlin post; but the purlin post being set square with the rafter, its *rise* is always the same as the *run* of the rafter, and its *run* is the same as the *rise* of the rafter.

Hence, for finding the length of a cripple stud, standing in any building between the rafter and the purlin post, at a certain horizontal distance from the top of the purlin plate, we have the following Rule: *Add the* RISE *of the roof in* RUNNING *the given distance to the* RUN *of the roof in* RISING *the given distance; the sum will give the length of the cripple stud.*

For example, in this plate, suppose the cripple stud *I* to be 18 inches from the top of the purlin plate, horizontal distance, then the rise of the roof on a quarter pitch in running 18 inches would be 9 inches, and the run of the roof in rising 18 inches would be 36 inches; so that the length of *I* is 45 inches. The stud marked *M* being 16 inches from *I*, the additional rise is 8 inches, and the additional run is 32 inches, so that *M* is 40 inches longer than *I*.

Note on Bevels.—The bevels in a frame of this kind are only four in number:—
1. The bevel of the upper end of the rafter.
2. The bevel of the foot of a rafter.
3. The bevel of the braces, &c—equal to 45 degrees.
4. The bevel of the upper end of the purlin post brace, always equal to the sum of the first and third. Balloon frames have but two bevels—the first and second above mentioned.

---

* Demonstrated as follows. The triangle ABC is similar to the triangle DEF, since the sides of the one are perpendicular to the sides of the other; consequently the angles opposite the perpendicular sides are equal. (Geom., Prop. 29.)

The side FE, in one triangle, is perpendicular to the side BC in the other; hence, the angle A = angle D. The angle A is the lower bevel of the rafters, and the angle D is the bevel of the cripple stud on the purlin post.

Plate 10.

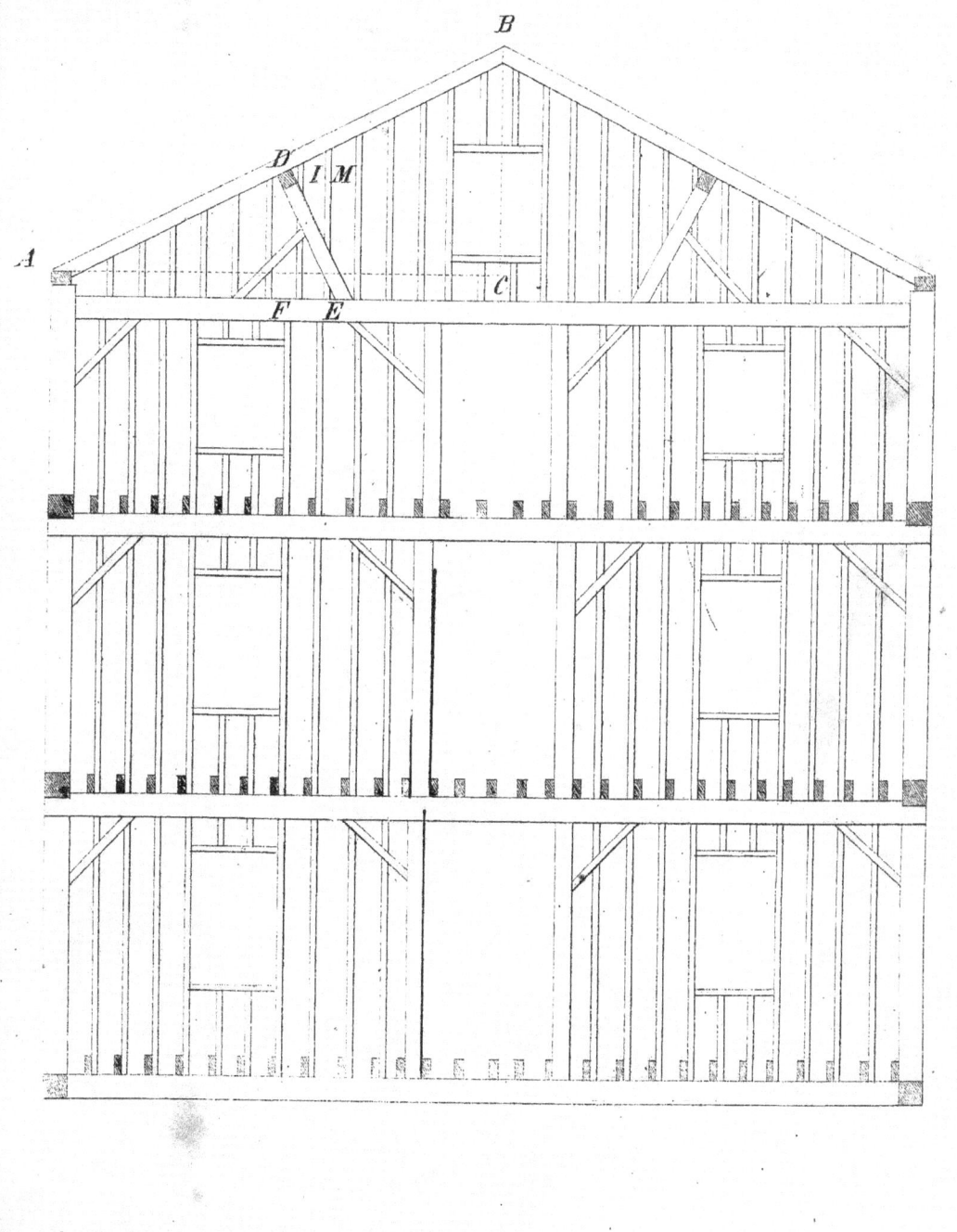

Plate II.

Fig. 1.

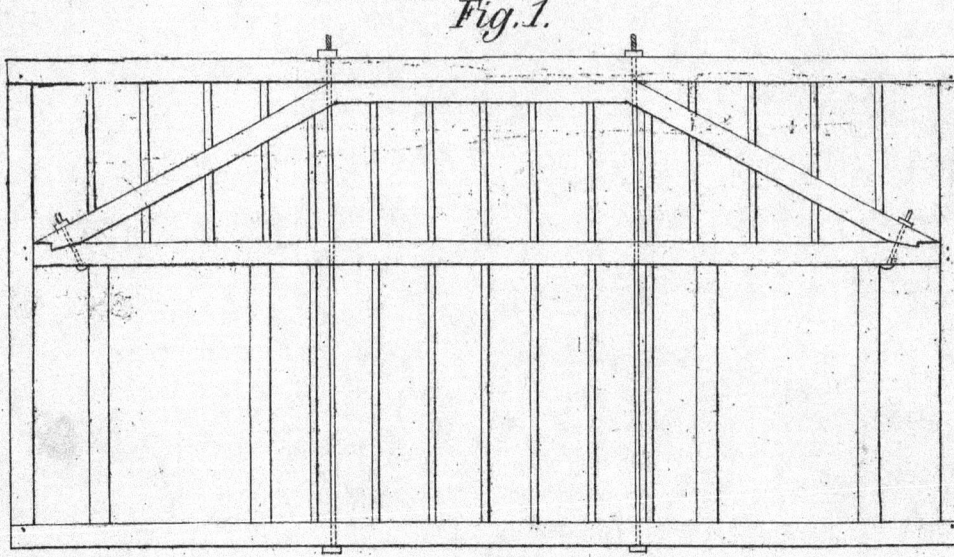

Scale 6 ft. to 1 inch.

Fig. 2.

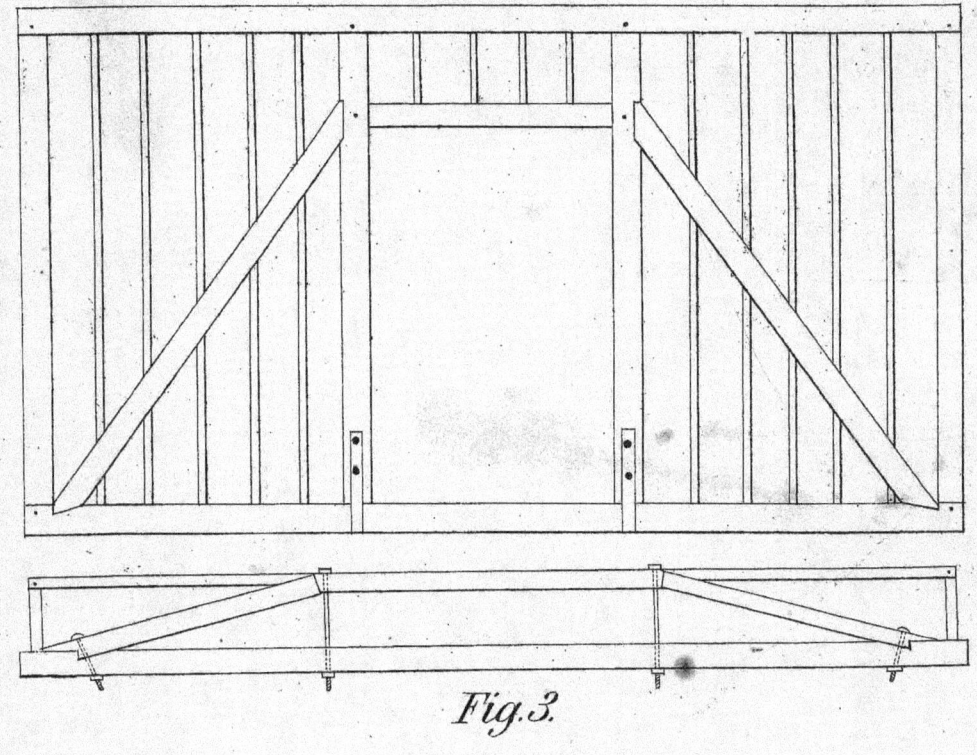

Fig. 3.

PLATE 11.

Plate 11 is designed to represent two modes of framing braces in a *self-supporting* or *trussed partition*. Where the span is considerable, there being no support beneath except the exterior wall, some mode of bracing is indispensable. These plans are exhibited as being *practicable and secure*.

The first plan gives opportunities for two or even three openings.

The second plan will be most convenient where only one opening is desired.

The size of these brace timbers should be in proportion to the width of the building, and the weight which the partition is to sustain. If they are ten or twelve inches square, they will safely sustain a brick wall built upon the partition.

Fig. 3 is designed to show the proper mode of trussing a beam over a barn floor, or in front of a church gallery, or any other situation where it is inconvenient to support it by posts.

PLATE 12.

SCARFING.

This Plate exhibits several designs for scarfing or splicing timber. The length of the splice should be about four times the thickness of the timber; and when the joint is beveling, it will be found the best and most expeditious way, first, to prepare an exact pattern of boards, and then to frame the timbers by the pattern: by this means a perfect joint can be made.

Straps and Bolts.

Fig. 4 is spliced by strapping pieces of plank upon the upper and lower sides of the joint, and securing them with bolts of $\frac{3}{4}$ inch or 1 inch in diameter, according to the size of the timber.

Figs. 5, 7, and 8, have iron straps bolted in a similar manner.

Fig. 9 exhibits a strong mode of splicing timbers where they are doubled throughout their whole length, for a very long span, such as roofs in churches.

Those styles which are numbered 1, 2, 7, and 5, are recommended as being the best in proportion to the cost.

Plate 12.

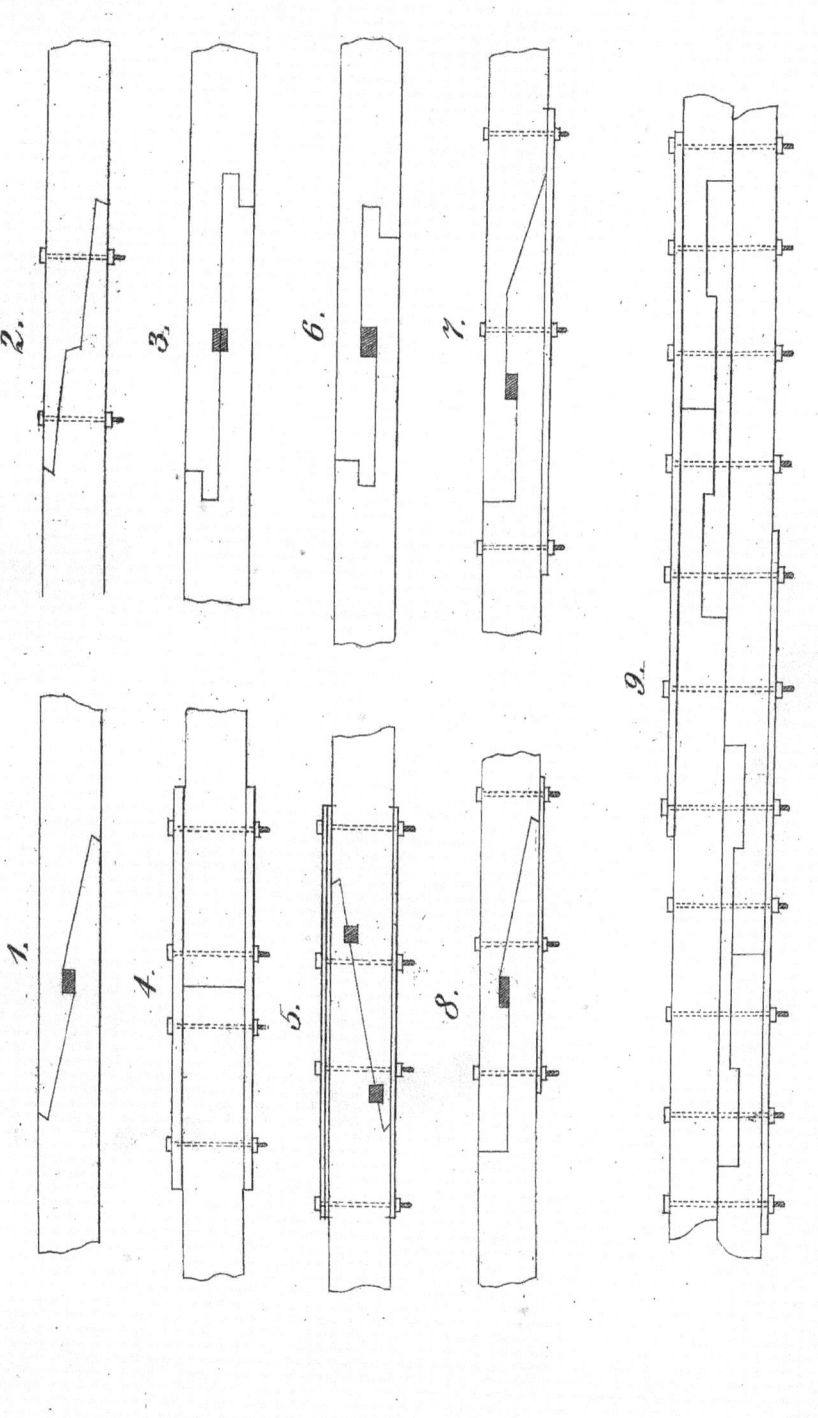

Plate 13.

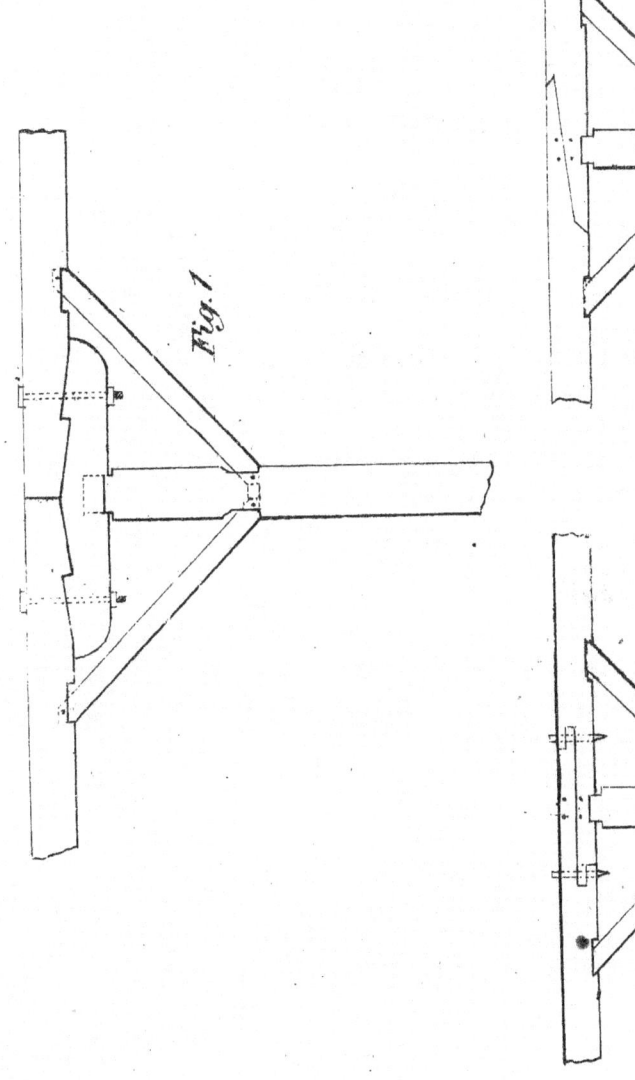
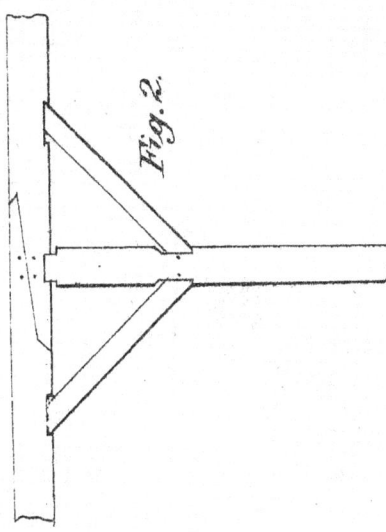
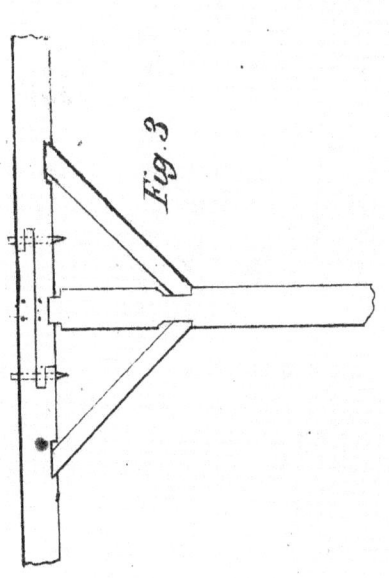

PLATE 13.

Scarfing, whenever it is practicable, should be made directly over a post, when a simple and inexpensive style, such as is exhibited in Plate 13, will be found sufficiently strong. Indeed, it is hardly possible to find a stronger mode of scarfing than that illustrated in Fig. 1; and yet, being supported by the post, the design is more simple than most of those represented in Plate 12.

In this design, the head of the post is framed into a bolster, which ought to be fully equal in size to the timber which it is required to support; in heavy frames it should be about 6 feet long, the braces being framed on a 4 feet run. The bolster is secured to the timber with inch bolts, as represented in the figure.

Fig. 1 also illustrates the proper mode of framing braces; the dotted lines show the form of the tenons, and the notchings in the post and the girder represent the facing of the mortices. These are usually notched-in half an inch at least, in order to give all possible support to the toe of the brace; and the measurement, for the length and the run of the braces, must be from the furthest point of the face of the mortice, inside of the notch, and not from the outside of the rough timber.

The shoulder of the post is also notched or *sized* into the bolster an inch, and the bolster is locked into the girder 2 inches; and, if the timber is 12 inches square, the shoulder of the post is 10 inches lower than it would be without any bolster; and the carpenter must, of course, make his brace mortices in the post, accordingly, 10 inches nearer the shoulder than usual.

Figs. 2 and 3 are designed to represent a less expensive mode of scarfing on posts. In these plans the tenons extend quite through, and are double-pinned to both timbers, as represented in the plate. This mode is sufficiently strong for scarfing plates and purlin plates.

PLATE 14.

FLOORS IN A BRICK BUILDING.

Plate 12, Fig. 1, exhibits the ground plan of one room, 18 feet wide. The joists are 2 by 10, 18 feet long.

Trimmer Joists.

Those marked A, B, and C, at each side of the fire-place, are called *trimmer joists*; they are 4 by 10; or they may be made by spiking two common joists together, as represented in the plate.

A course of *bridging* is represented at D, as described in Plate 6.

Fig. 2 and Fig. 5 exhibit the method of framing the tenons of the common joists.

Fig. 3 shows the mode of framing together the trimmer joists at the corners of the hearth

Fig. 4 shows the beveled ends of the joists where they are set into the brick wall. They are beveled in the manner represented, that the springing of the joists may not endanger the wall; and, in case of fire, the joists may burn and fall out without destroying the wall.

Plate 14.

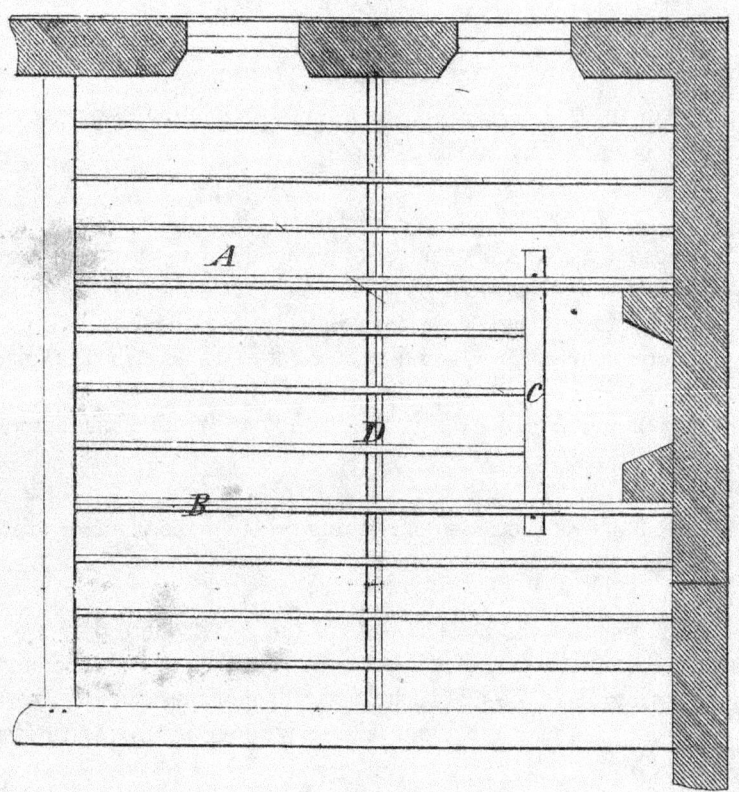

Fig. 1.

Fig. 3.    Fig. 2.

Fig. 4. 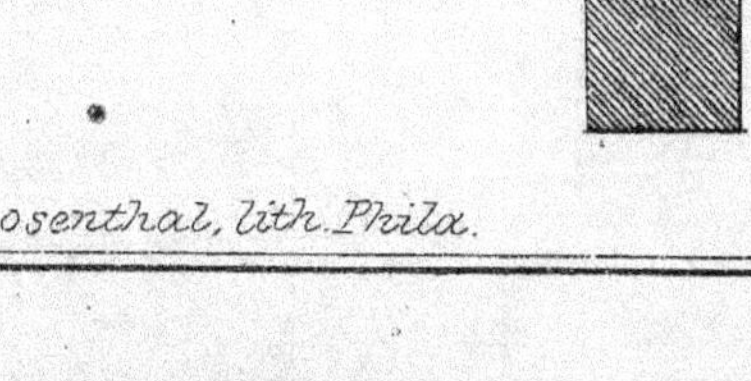   Fig. 5.

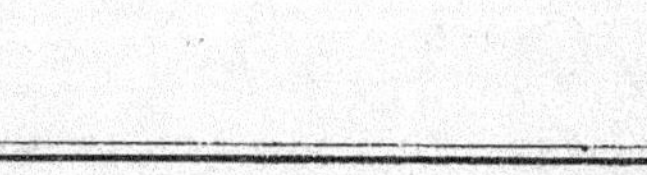

L. N. Rosenthal, lith. Phila.

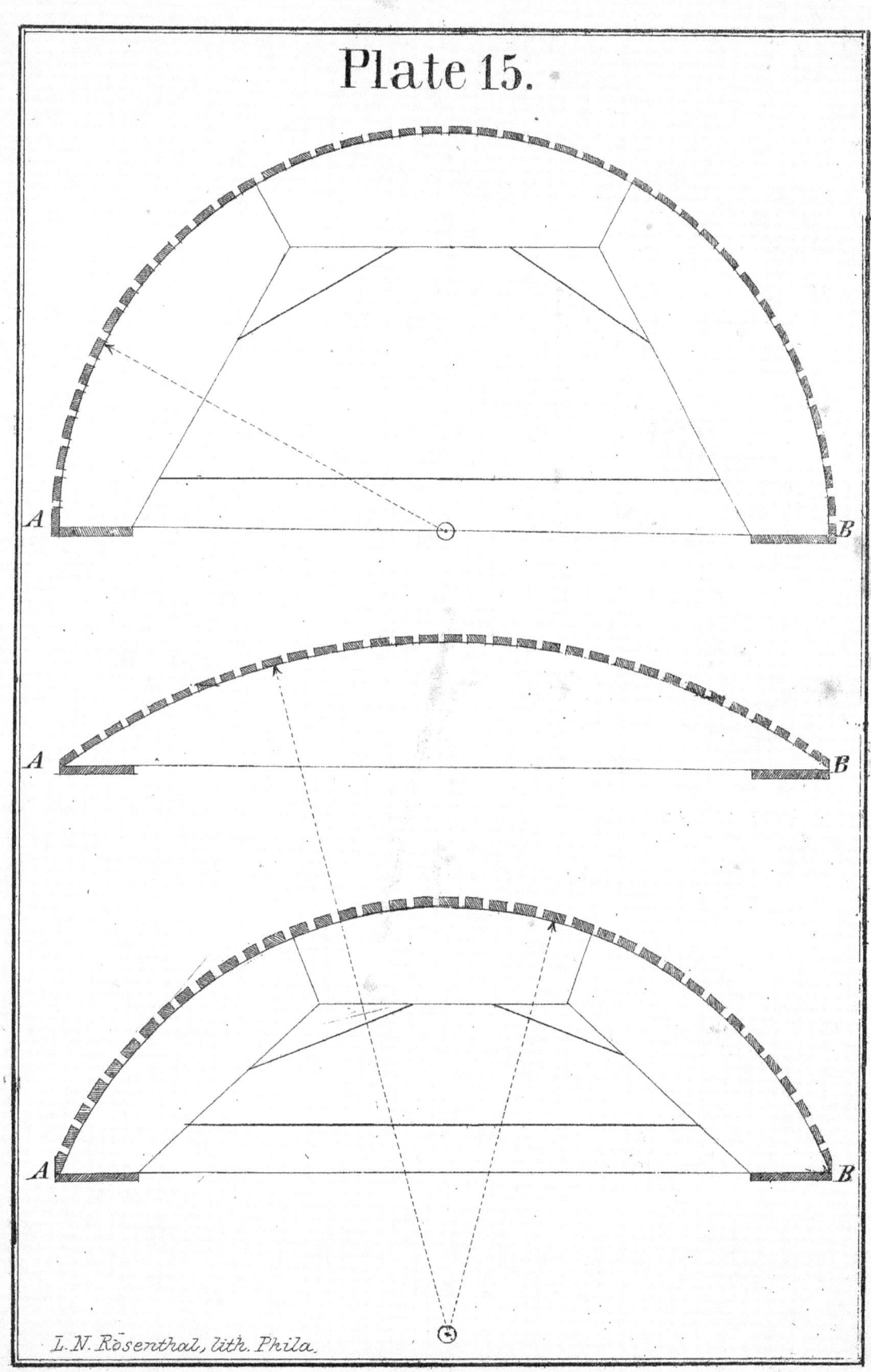

Plate 15.

PLATE 15.

CIRCULAR CENTRES.

Plate 15 exhibits several designs, more or less convex, for the construction of centres, which are skeletons used by stone and brick masons to build an arch upon, but which are to be taken away when the arch is sprung and the mortar set.

First, draw the line AB upon a floor, two inches less than the width of the skeleton required, and take OA as a radius, and describe the semi-circumference. Inch boards are then to be fitted to this curved line, and their ends beveled to fit each other, as represented in the Plate. The bevel is determined by simply drawing a straight line from any point of the curve to the central point O. Other boards are then to be nailed over the joints, on the inside of these; and the long brace AB nailed at each end at the bottom.

Having prepared the other end of the skeleton in the same manner, strips of boards, an inch thick, two inches wide, and of a length equal to the thickness of the wall, are nailed upon their convex edges, as represented.

Should the arch have more than 12 feet span, it would be proper to use thicker boards; but for any thing less than 12 feet, inch boards are amply sufficient.

PLATE 16.

ELLIPTICAL CENTRES.

This Plate illustrates the manner of constructing elliptical centres. The elliptical curve is described most accurately by means of a *trammel*, the construction and use of which are explained in Plate 2, page 20.

In order to describe the curve for these centres, take AB equal to the span of the arch, less 2 inches, and set the trammel so that the intersection of the arms will fall upon O, the middle point of AB. Then set the pin B, so that PB will equal the height of the arch less 1 inch; and set the pin C so that PC will equal AO.

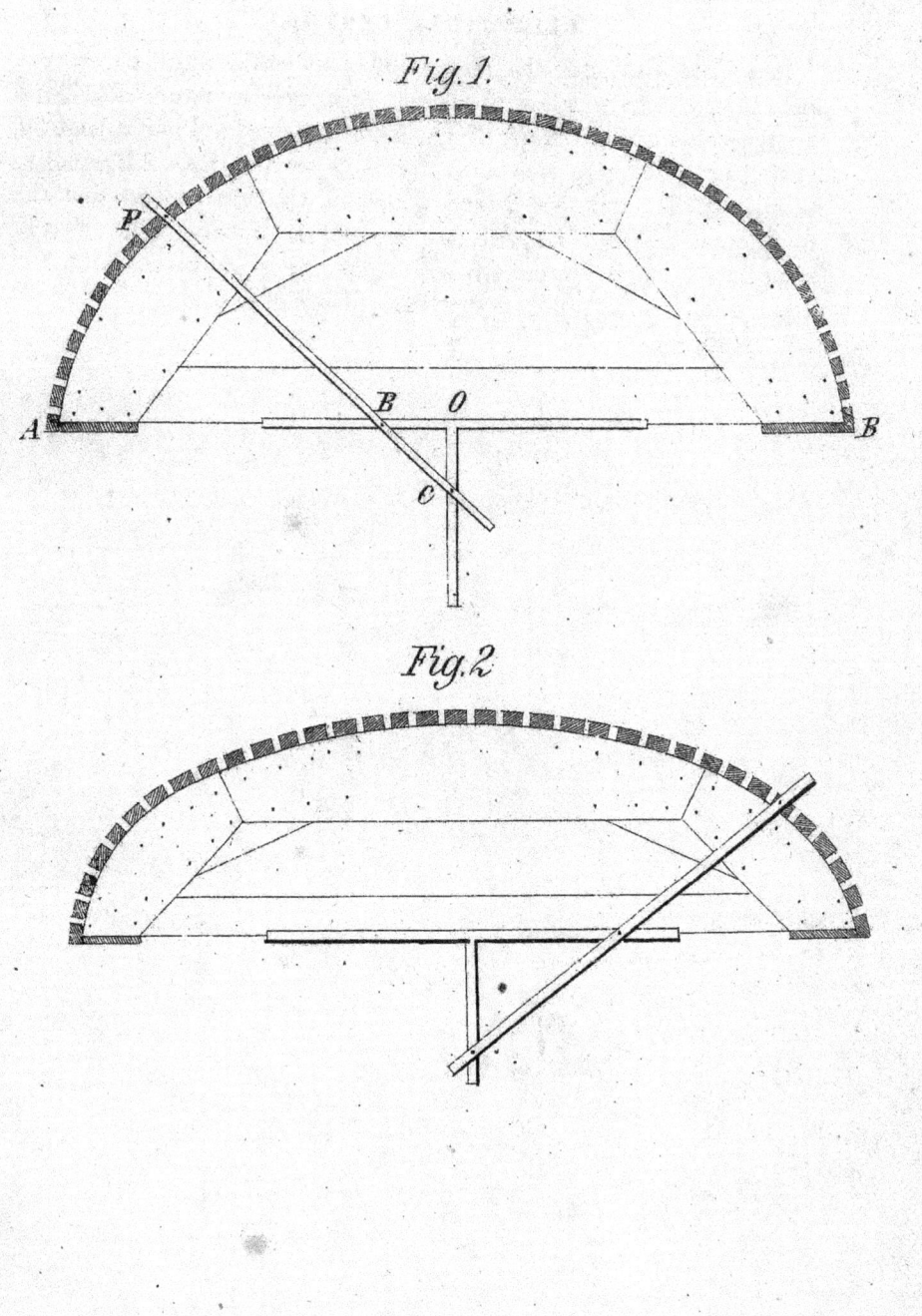

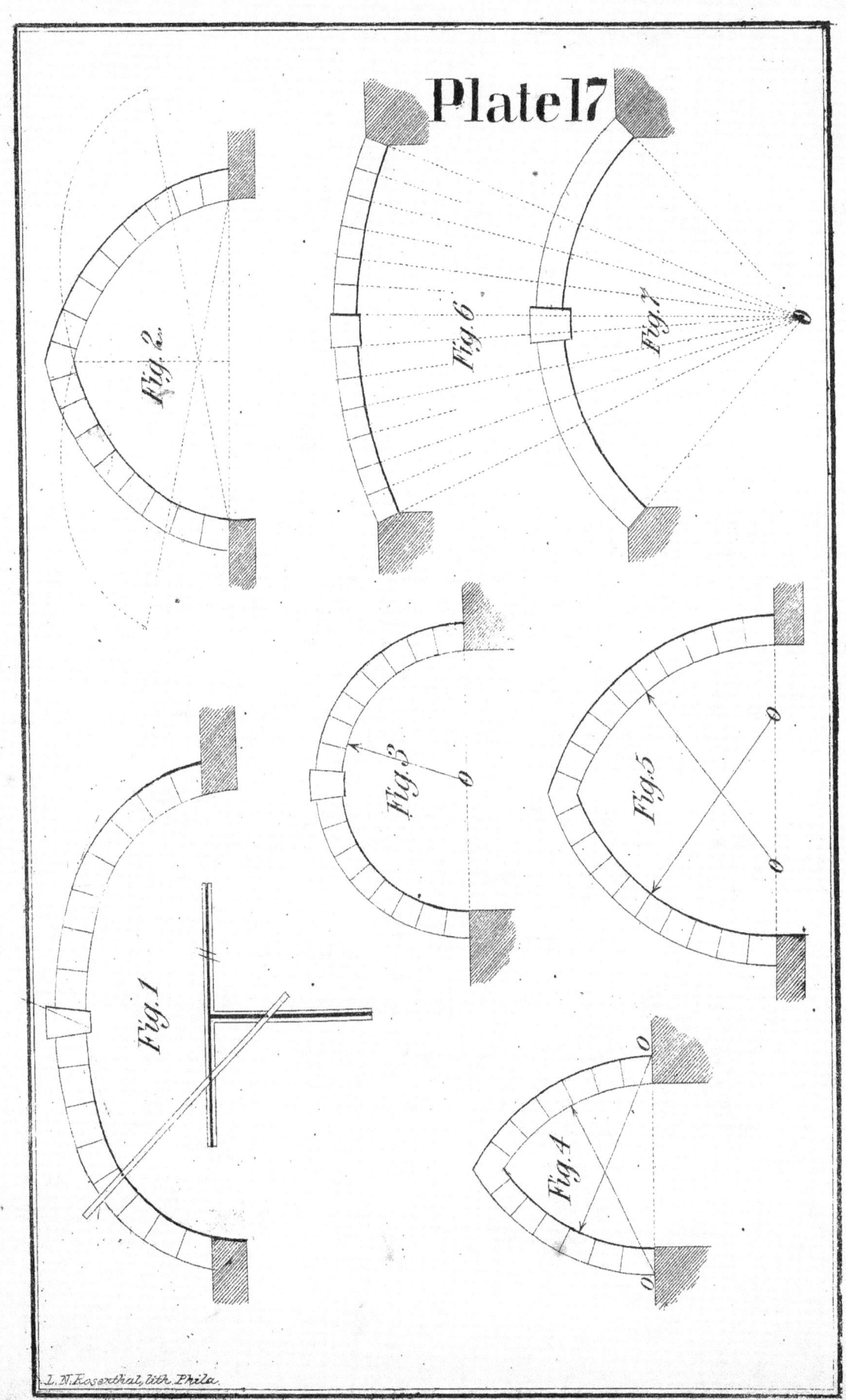

PLATE 17.

ARCHES.

It is also the business of the carpenter to prepare patterns for stone-cutters, by which they are to cut their stones to fit arches of any desired form. This Plate exhibits seven different styles of arches, with the most accurate and convenient modes of drawing them, and of dividing them into proper sections or patterns for the arch-stones.

Fig. 1 represents an elliptical arch, drawn by means of a trammel, as has been already described. The arch is divided into blocks of proper form and size, by first dividing the curve into any desired number of equal spaces; then, wherever a joint is required, first draw a tangent to the curve at that point, and then a line perpendicular to this tangent will divide the arch properly.

Fig. 2 exhibits the Tudor arch, drawn in two rampant semi-elliptical curves, as represented in the Plate. The same rule is to be observed as before for finding the joints of this arch, and for dividing it correctly into proper patterns.

Fig. 3 is a semicircular arch. This is most easily and correctly jointed by drawing a radius from the centre O to any point of the curve where a joint is desired.

Fig. 4 is a Gothic arch, described by two equal radii from the points O, O, as centres, and jointed from the same points.

Fig. 5 is so similar to the last, as to require no further description.

Figs. 6 and 7 exhibit two depressed segmental arches of the same span, but representing different degrees of curvature, one being drawn with a longer radius than the other, and both jointed by radii drawn from the common centre O.

PLATE 18.

HIP ROOFS.

Plate 18, Fig. 1, exhibits the plan of a hip roof in a building 50 feet long and 40 feet wide, the rise of the roof being 5 inches to the foot. AB, CD, and EF, are the upper girders, which are trussed for supporting the roof, with short principal rafters and straining beams, as represented in the Plate at CD.

GH, IH, KL, and ML, are the hip rafters, and HL the ridge pole. The purlin plates are placed upon the principal rafters, and the straining beams are framed on a level with the purlin plates, so that the end ones may answer the double purpose of straining beams and purlin plates also.

The lengths* and bevels of the common rafters, in the middle of the building, the upper ends of which rest against the ridge pole, are found as usual in common roofs. (Table No. 1.)

Hip Rafters.

The *length* of the hip rafters is given in the Hip Rafter Table, (No. 2, p. 119) where the rule for obtaining it is fully explained.

In addition to the two bevels common to all rafters, namely, the upper end bevel and the lower end bevel, hip rafters have two other bevels, which are the *side bevel*, as it is called, being the angle which the two hip rafters make with each other at their intersection, and the *backing*, which is the angle made by the intersection of the side roof with the end roof.

Side Bevel of the Hip Rafters.

It is evident that if there were no pitch to the roof, this bevel would be 45 degrees, since the two hip rafters would be perfectly square with each other; but as soon as the roof begins to rise, the hip rafters are no longer square with each other, but begin to approach a parallel,

---

* Throughout this work, the length of rafters is computed from the upper and outer corners of the plates to the very peak of the roof, without allowances for the projection of the rafters or the thickness of the ridge poles. In case the building has a ridge pole, therefore, it will be necessary to deduct one half the thickness of it from the length as given, measuring for this deduction square from the down bevel, and not lengthwise of the rafter.

Plate 18.

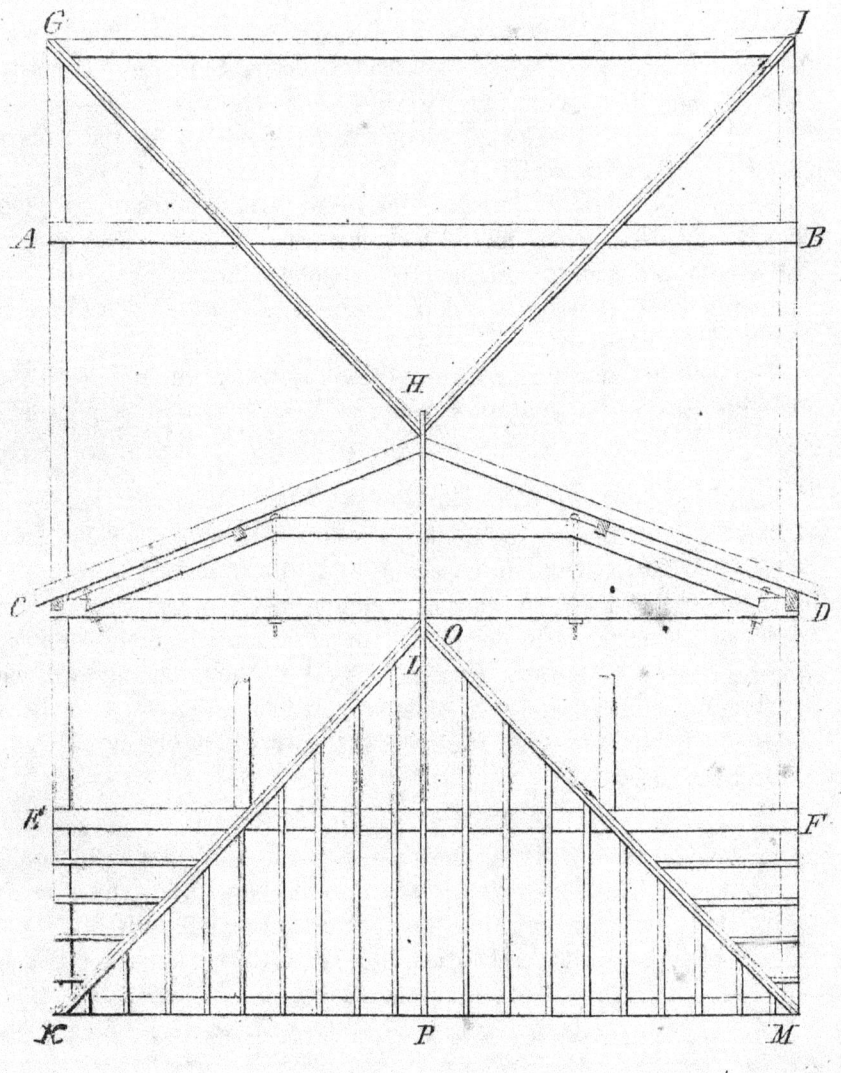

HIP ROOFS.

till, in a very steep roof, as that of a tower or steeple, they are nearer parallel than square with each other. The side bevel, therefore, is always greater than 45 degrees, and is obtained from the square by taking the length of the hip rafter on the blade, and its run on the tongue; the blade then shows the side bevel of the hip rafter required.

Down Bevel of the Hip Rafters.

The upper end bevel is commonly called, in hip rafters, the *down bevel*. It is always square with the lower end bevel, the one being the complement of the other. This bevel varies with the pitch of the roof; for the pitch of the hip rafter always has the same proportion to the pitch of the common rafter, that the *run* of the common rafter has to the *run* of the hip rafter, or that the side of a square has to its diagonal; for, if we let O represent the foot of the perpendicular let fall from L upon the middle of the girder, CD, then ODPM is a square, of which OD, the run of a common rafter, is the side, and OM, the run of the hip rafter, is the diagonal. Now, it is a well-known principle in mathematics, that *the side of any square is proportioned to its diagonal, as* ONE *is to the* SQUARE ROOT OF TWO, (Prop. XXIV., *Cor.*); or, as 1 is to 1.4142; or, as 12 inches are to 17 inches *nearly*. When the common rafter, therefore, has 5 inches rise to 12 inches run, the hip rafter of the same roof has 5 inches rise to 17 inches run; and when the common rafter has 6 inches rise to 12 inches run, the hip rafter has 6 inches rise to 17 inches run; &c.

From these demonstrations we derive the following Rule for finding the down bevel and the lower end bevel of the hip rafters. *Take 17 inches on the blade of the square for the run, and the rise of the roof to the foot on the tongue.* The tongue will give the down bevel, or upper end bevel, and the blade the lower end bevel.

Backing of the Hip Rafters.

This is found on the square by taking the length of the hip rafter on the blade, and the rise of the roof on the tongue; the bevel of the tongue will be the backing required. For illustration, in this building the length of the hip rafters, as given in the Table, equals $29\frac{1}{2}$ feet *nearly*, and the rise of the roof is $8\frac{1}{3}$ feet. Take proportional parts of each on the square, and the tongue will give the backing; that is, place the square upon a strait edge, with the blade at the $14\frac{3}{4}$ inch mark, and the tongue at the $4\frac{1}{4}$ inch mark, and draw a scratch along the tongue; then set a bevel square to the angle which this scratch makes with the straight edge, and it is the backing required.

Lengths and Bevels of the Jack Rafters.

Since the pitch of the jack rafters is the same as that of the common rafters, the longest jack rafter, the upper end of which rests against the end of the ridge pole, is of the same length as the common rafters, as given in the Common Rafter Table, less half the thickness of the hip rafters at their side bevel on the ridge pole. The difference in length between the longest jack rafter and the next one, or between any two adjacent ones, is equal to their distance apart, added to the *gain* of the rafter in running that distance.

For example, in this building, the width being 40 feet, the *run* of the jack rafter is 20 feet, or 240 inches; and its *length*, on a pitch of 5 inches rise to the foot, is 260 inches; therefore, its *gain* is 20 inches in running 20 feet, or an inch to a foot. The jack rafters being 2 feet apart, the difference in length between any two adjacent ones is, therefore, 2 feet 2 inches.

Or, the length of the shorter jack rafters may be obtained from that of the longest one, by dividing the length of the longest one by the number of spaces between the longest one and the corner of the building; the quotient will be the length of the shortest one, and it will be also the difference between any two adjacent ones.

The *down bevel* and the *lower end bevel* are the same as the upper and lower end bevels of the common rafters.

The *side bevel* of the jack rafters is always more than 45°, for a similar reason as that given in the description of the side bevel of the hip rafters; and, since all the jack rafters have the same pitch as the common rafters, we have the following

Rule for obtaining the side bevel of the jack rafters.—Take the length of a common rafter on the blade of a square, and its run on the tongue—or proportional parts of each. The bevel on the blade is the side bevel of all the jack rafters in the frame.

Or, take the length of the longest jack rafter on the blade, and half the width of the building on the tongue, or proportional parts of each, and the bevel on the blade will be the required side bevel.

Remark.—In a hip roof which is perfectly square, the hip rafters need have no side bevel; for two of them can be cut of full length, and set up, opposite each other first, with their down bevels resting full against each other like common rafters; the other two hip rafters can then be set against these, having been cut off half their thickness shorter than the full length.

Plate 19.

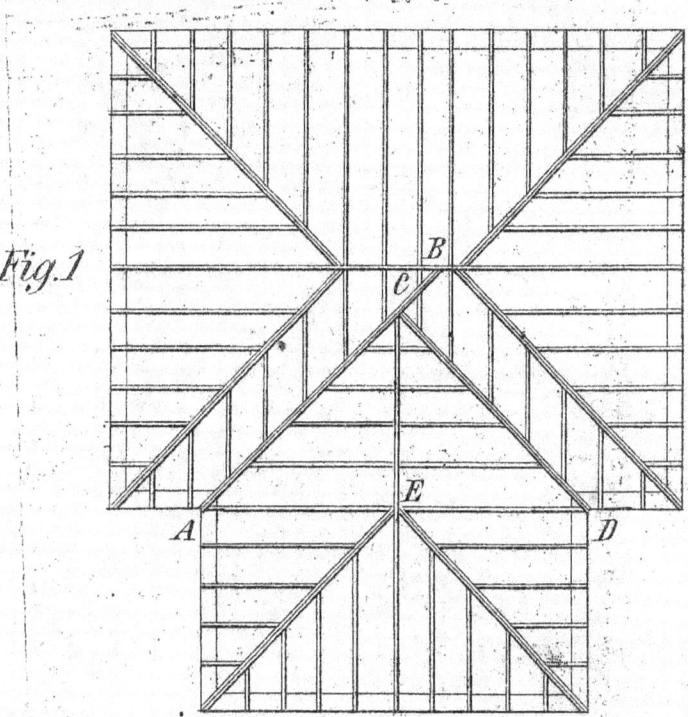

Fig.1

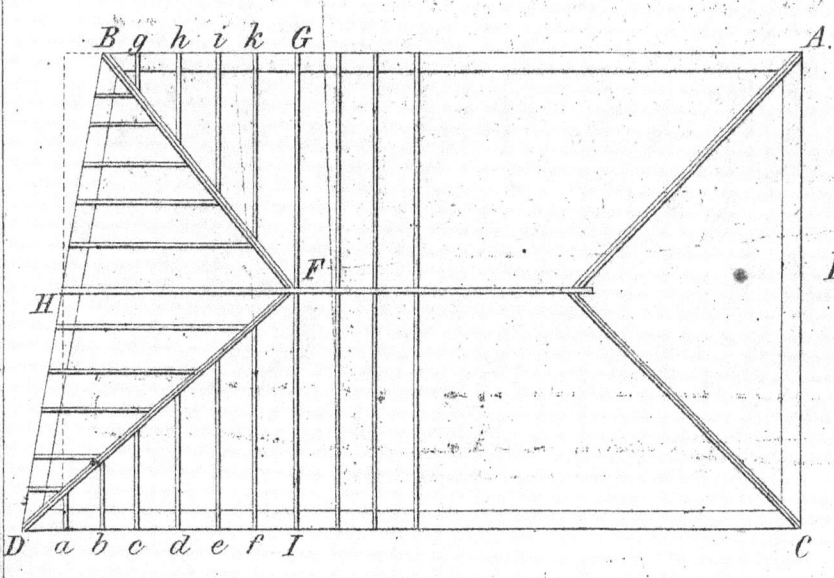

Fig.2

Scale 10 ft. to the inch.

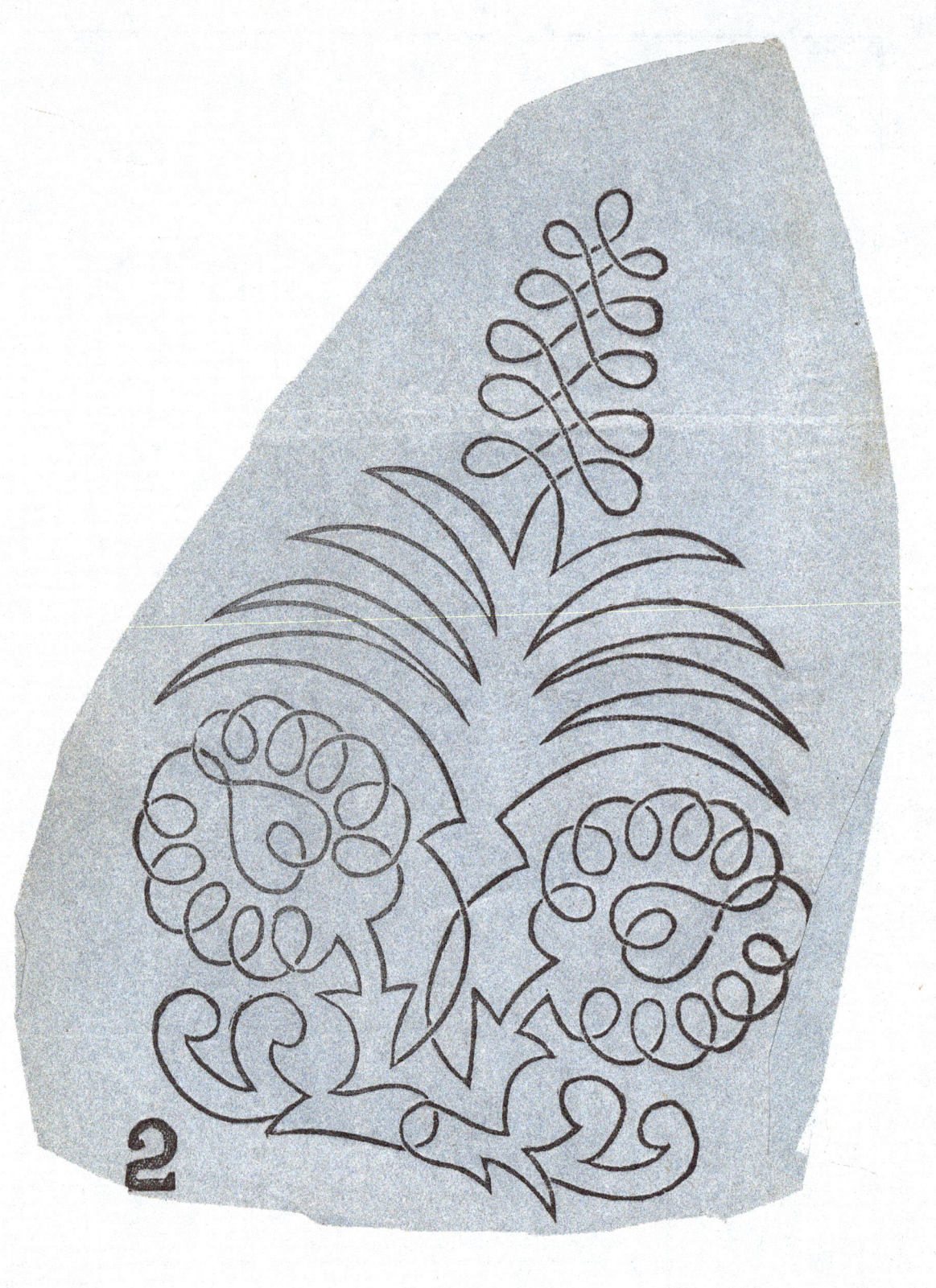

PLATE 19.

HIPS AND VALLEYS.

Plate 19, Fig. 1, represents the hip roof of a building consisting of a main portion and a wing, the walls of the wing being of the same height as those of the main building. The main building being 24 by 30 feet, and the wing 10 by 20 feet, the roof of the wing being of the same pitch, will not rise as high as that of the other part.

The timbers AB and CD at the intersection of these roofs are called *valley rafters*. The upper end of the first one, AB, is extended to the ridge pole of the main building; the other valley rafter is supported by the first one, by being spiked to it at their intersection at C. From that point of intersection, a ridge pole extends to the intersection of the end hip rafters at E. This ridge pole is equal in length to the whole width of the wing; the valley rafter and hip rafter on each side being parallel with each other.

The lengths and bevels of the various rafters are found as explained in the preceding Plate.

TRAPEZOIDAL HIP ROOFS.

Fig. 2 exhibits the plan of a hip roof for a building constructed in the form of an irregular square, or trapezoid; the side CD being 4 feet longer than the side AB, the width 24 feet and the rise 5 inches to the foot.

The length and bevels of the common rafters and of the hip rafters on the square end of the frame are obtained in the same manner as described, in the regular hip roof. The lengths and bevels of the two hip rafters BF and DF on the beveled end of the frame are unlike each other, and unlike those on the square end, one being longer and the other shorter than those. As such buildings are comparatively rare, it has not been deemed necessary to encumber this work with a table for such rafters, but the facts and principles applicable to such frames are here stated.

Lengths of the Irregular Hip Rafters.

If this end of the building were square, then BG and DI would each of them be equal to half the width of the building, or 12 feet;

but since one side of the building is 4 feet shorter than the other side, the short side is 2 feet less than 12, and the long side 2 feet more than 12; or BG equals 10 feet, and DI equals 14 feet.

The length of the common rafters GF and IF is found by the table to equal 13 feet; and the two triangles GFB and IFD being right-angled, we are now furnished with the means of finding the lengths of the two hip rafters BF and DF, by the use of that familiar principle in mathematics, that *in every right-angled triangle the square of the hypotenuse is equal to the sum of the squares of the other two sides.* (Part I., Prop. XXIV.) For in the right-angled triangle GFB, we have the side GB equal to 10 feet, which we reduce to inches, to secure greater accuracy in calculation. GB then equals 120 inches, and GF, a common rafter, equals 13 feet or 156 inches. The square of 120 is 14,400, and the square of 156 is 24,336; the sum of these squares is 38,736, which is the same as the square of the hypotenuse BF; and by extracting the square root of 38,736 inches, we have 195 inches and 81 hundredths of an inch, or 16 feet 4.81 inches, as the length of the hip rafter BF.

The length of DF is found in a similar manner from the triangle IFD, DI being 14 feet or 168 inches, the square of which is 28,224, to which add the square of IF, equal to that of GF, found above to be 24,336. The sum of these squares is 52,560 inches, of which the square root is 229.25 inches, or 19 feet 1.25 inches, the true length of the longest hip rafter.

Bevels of the Irregular Hip Rafters.

The *down bevel* and the *lower end bevel* of these irregular hip rafters, like those of all other rafters, are square with each other: and are found together on the square by taking the *run* on the blade and the *rise* on the tongue; the tongue will give the down bevel, and the blade the lower end bevel.

Note.—Take the square of BG, and the square of DI, respectively; add to each the square of half the width of the building; extract the square root of each of these sums, and they will give the *runs* of BF and DF, respectively.

Thus, the square of BG, 10 feet, or 120 inches, is 14,400 inches; the square of DI, 14 feet, or 168 inches, is 28,224 inches; and the square of half the width of the building, 12 feet, or 144 inches, is 20,736 inches; this added to 14,400 is 35,136 inches, the square root of which is 187.44 inches, or 15 feet 7.44 inches, which is the *run* of BF.

Again, 20,736 added to 28,224 equals 48,960, the square root of which is 221.26 inches, or 18 feet 5.26 inches, the *run* of DF.

The *side bevel* of irregular hip rafters is obtained by adding together the distance from the foot of the hip rafter to the foot of the first common

TRAPEZOIDAL HIP ROOFS. 75

rafter, and the gain of the hip rafter; then take this sum on the tongue of a square, and half the width of the building on the blade; and the tongue will give the side bevel required.

Backing of Hip Rafters on Trapezoidal and other Irregular Roofs.

As the oblique angles of trapezoidal and other irregular buildings are liable to many variations, so the backing of the hip rafters must also vary on different roofs. The simplest and most practical manner of finding these backings, when thus irregular, is to take a small square block, and bevel one end of it to the same bevel as the lower end of the hip rafter in question. Then place this beveled end upon the plates, just as the hip rafter is to be placed, at the oblique corner of the building, and draw a pencil line on the under side of the block, along the upper and outer edges of the plates, till they meet at the corner; these lines will be the bevel of the backing required. And then the block can be worked off to the lines, and a bevel square set to the angle thus formed, by which the hip rafter itself can then be beveled.

Length of the Jack Rafters.

First. Of those on the long side of the building, between D and I. In the triangle DFI, the jack rafter f, being parallel with the base FI, has the same proportion to FI that Df has to DI (Geom., Props. XXV. & XXVII.); and in order to find the length of the jack rafters coming between I and D, we have only to divide IF by the number of rafters required from IF to the corner inclusively, and the quotient will be the difference between any two of them, and will equal also the length of the shortest one. Since it is 14 feet from I to the corner of the building, and the rafters are 2 feet apart, it will require 7 rafters, including IF. We therefore divide IF, 13 feet, by 7, and have 1 foot $10\frac{3}{7}$ inches for the difference between IF and f, and also between f and e; or, what is equally true, we can take this number, 1 foot $10\frac{3}{7}$ inches, as the length of a; double this, or 3 feet $8\frac{4}{7}$ inches, for the length of b; three times this number, or 5 feet $6\frac{6}{7}$ inches, for the length of c; 7 feet $5\frac{1}{7}$ inches, the length of d; 9 feet $3\frac{3}{7}$ inches, the length of e; 11 feet $1\frac{5}{7}$ inches, the length of f; and 13 feet the length of IF: proving the calculation to be correct. It will be most convenient in practice to cut the longest ones first, that the short pieces of stuff may be worked in to better advantage.

Second. In the same manner obtain the difference between GF and *k*, on the other side of the building, by dividing GF, 13 feet, by 5, the number of rafters required in GB; 13 feet divided by 5 equals 2 feet $7\frac{1}{5}$ inches; this is at once the length of *g* and the difference between any two adjacent rafters between B and G.

Third. Of those on the end of the building. Divide the length of HF by 6, which is the number of rafters required between HF and each corner of the building, including HF. HF equals the length of a common rafter, less 2 inches—the bevel of the hip rafters —or 12 feet 10 inches, which, divided by 6, equals 2 feet $1\frac{2}{3}$ inches, the length of each of the short rafters on the end, and also the difference between HF and the jack rafters on each side of HF.

Side Bevels of the Jack Rafters on the Sides of the Frame.

It is evident that, if the roof were horizontal, this bevel would be found on the square, by taking half the width of the building on the blade, and the distance from the corner of the building to the foot of the first common rafter on the tongue; but when the roof begins to pitch, this bevel will be too short; and the relation of the pitch of the roof to the length of the common rafter is such, that the side bevel of the jack rafters is obtained with perfect accuracy, by taking *the length of the common rafter on the blade, and the distance from D to I and from B to G, respectively, on the tongue*—the blade will give the side bevels required.

The *down bevels* and lower end bevels of these jack rafters on the sides of the frame are the same as those of the common rafters, since they have the same pitch that the common rafters have.

Side Bevels of the Jack Rafters on the Slant End of the Frame.

For a similar reason assigned above, *add to BG the gain of a common rafter in running the length of GB. Then take this sum on the blade of a square, and half the width of the building on the tongue,* and it will give the side bevel of the end rafters which are nearest BG. In like manner, add to DI the gain of a common rafter in running the length of DI. Take this sum on the blade, and half the width of the building on the tongue, and it will give the bevel required of those rafters nearest DI.

For illustration, BG equals 10 feet; as the common rafters are 13 feet long, in running 12 feet, they gain an inch in running a foot. So, in running 10 feet, a rafter would gain 10 inches. We therefore take a certain proportional part of 10 feet 10 inches on the blade of a square, say 10¾ inches, and the same proportional of half the width of the building, say 12 inches, on the tongue; the bevel of the blade is the side bevel for all those jack rafters on the end of the frame which are nearest GB, or which rest against BF.

So, also, DI equals 14 feet, to which add 14 inches; hence, take 15⅛ inches on the blade, and 12 inches on the tongue; the bevel on the blade will be the side bevels of those jack rafters on the end of the frame nearest DI, which rest against the hip rafter DF.

Down Bevel of the Jack Rafters on the Beveled End of the Frame.

In order to obtain these bevels and the corresponding lower end bevels with perfect accuracy, it is necessary to obtain them for each rafter separately, for there are no two of them which have the same pitch. In order to ascertain with ease what this pitch and the corresponding bevels are, it is necessary to suppose all these end rafters to be produced beyond where they now rest on the hip rafters, and all to rest upon a common ridge pole PR, which is drawn through the point F, and extends on a level with F directly over the points G and I. These rafters would then have each one the same pitch they now have, since we have not supposed their *direction* changed, but their *length* only. Now, however, the rise is 5 feet for each one, and their run can easily be computed from the length of BG; for the run of the one nearest B is 4 inches more than BG, or 10 feet 4 inches; that of the next one, 4 inches more, or 10 feet 8 inches; &c.

Now, in order to obtain the down bevel and the lower end bevel of any rafter, we take the run on the blade of a square, and the rise on the tongue.

The measurements of these bevels are therefore as follows:

5 inches on the tongue for each of them, and 10¼ inches, 10⅔ inches, 11 inches, 11⅓ inches, 11⅔ inches, 12 inches, 12⅓ inches, 12⅔ inches, 13 inches, 13⅓ inches, 13⅔ inches, respectively, on the blade.

PLATE 20.

OCTAGONAL AND HEXAGONAL ROOFS.

Plate 20, Fig. 1, is designed to exhibit the proper mode of framing the roof of a building, the ground plan of which is a *regular octagon*. This style of building having become quite common, a Rafter Table (No. 3) has been prepared, which will be found very useful and convenient, as it gives at one view the precise lengths of the longest hip rafters and the longest jack rafters. In the introduction or explanation of the table, full instruction and demonstrations are given for enabling the intelligent mechanic to test these calculations, or to extend and apply them to roofs of other dimensions.

Length of the Hip Rafters.

The length given in the Table is that of the first pair, and is calculated from the outer and upper corner of the plates, at their intersection with each other, to the very central point or apex of the roof.

One of the first pair having been cut off of the above length and of the proper down bevel, the length of the second pair is obtained from this one, by taking off from this one half its thickness, measured back square from the down bevel; and the length of the third and fourth pairs, by taking off in like manner two thirds its thickness, or more accurately, $\frac{17}{24}$ of its thickness, since 17 is half the diagonal of a square, the side of which is 24. (See Prop. XXIV., *Cor.*)

Bevels of the Hip Rafters.

The *down bevel*, and lower end bevel, are found as usual, that is, by the run of the rafter and its rise, on the square. (The *run of the hip rafter* is half the diagonal width of the building. See Explanation of Octagonal Hip Roof Table.)

The first and second pairs of hip rafters have no *side bevel*, since, in raising the frame, the first pair, HI, have their ends resting against each other, as in common rafters. The second pair, AP, are next raised at right angles with the first, and their ends resting square against the first. The third and fourth pairs have their side bevels

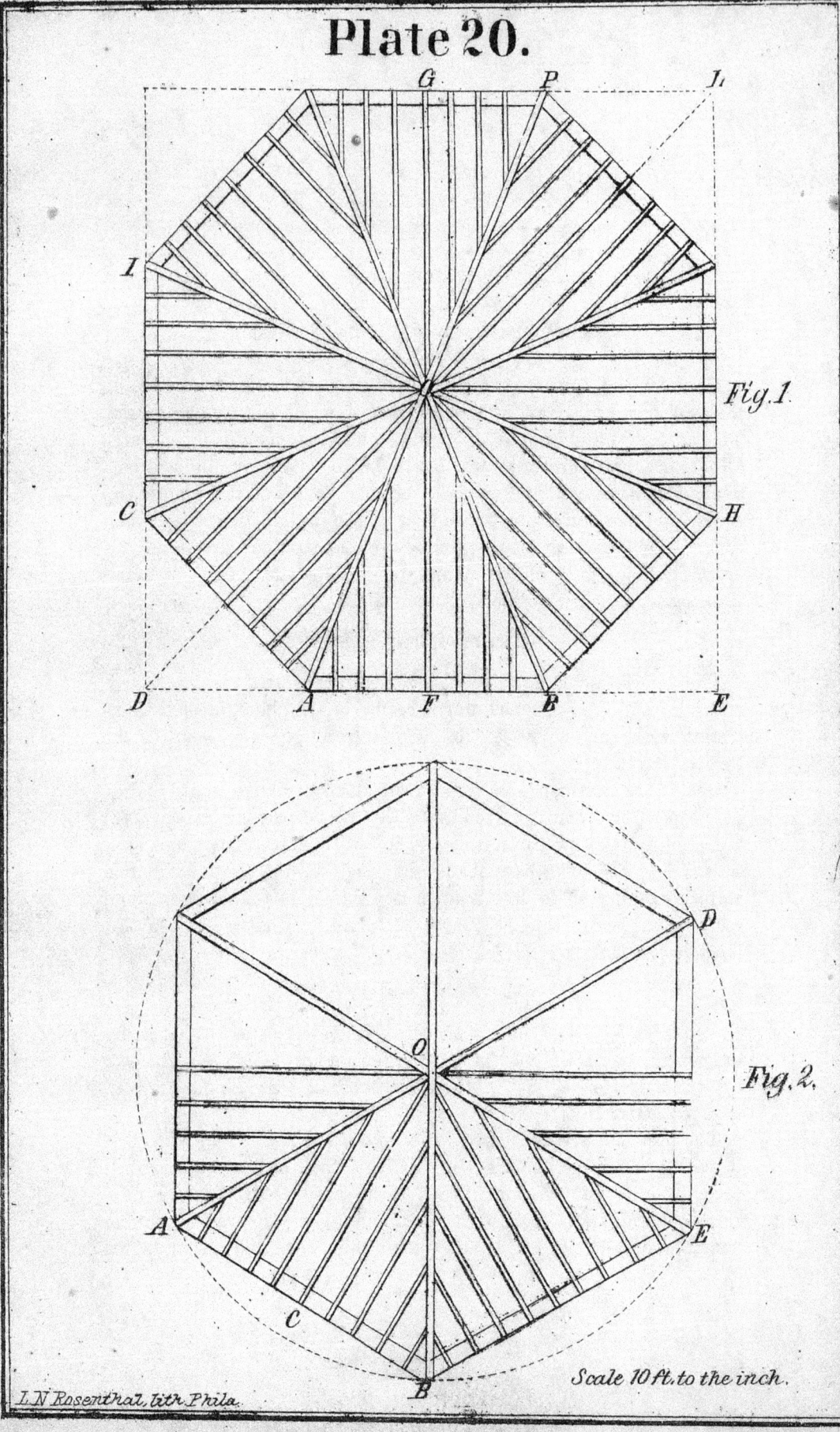

cut on both sides of the upper end; and that bevel is found by taking the length of the rafter and its run on the square.

The *backing* of the *hip rafter* is obtained on the square by taking $\frac{5}{12}$ of its *rise* on the tongue, and its *length* on the blade.

Length of the Jack Rafters.

The length of the middle jack rafters is given in the Table. Having found this, in order to obtain the length of the shortest one, proceed as directed in the article on trapezoidal hip roofs; that is, divide the length of the longest one by the number of rafters required between that and the corner inclusively—the quotient will be the length of the shortest one, and also the difference between any two adjacent ones.

THE BEVELS OF THE JACK RAFTERS are obtained on the same principle as those in common hip roofs.

The *down bevel* is found on the square by taking the length and the run of the middle jack rafter; and the *side bevel* by taking the length of this rafter and half the side of the building.

Fig. 2 represents the roof of a building, the ground plan of which is a *regular hexagon*.

Width of the Building.

In every regular hexagon the *side* is equal to the radius of the circumscribed circle; and the *diagonal width* is equal to the diameter of the circumscribed circle, or twice the side. If we let O' represent the foot of the perpendicular let fall from O, then AB and BE are each equal to AO' and BO', and AD is equal to twice AB.*

Half the *square width of the building* is found by subtracting from the square of the side, the square of half the side, and extracting the square root of the difference: since, in the right-angled triangle CO'B, $CO'^2 = BO'^2 - CB^2$. The side of this building being supposed to be 20 feet, we have the square of $20 = 400$, and the square of $\frac{20}{2} = 100$; their difference is 300 feet, the square root of which is 17.35 feet, or 17 feet 4.2 inches, which is half the width of the building, or the run of the middle jack rafter

The Length of the Rafter

Must be computed as explained in the Introduction to the Rafter

---

*. See Geom., Prop. XXXI.

Table; that is, to say, every rafter is the hypotenuse of a right-angled triangle, of which its *run* and its *rise* are the other two sides. The square of the length is therefore equal to the sum of the squares of the run and the rise.

In this Fig. the roof is supposed to rise 3 inches to the foot. The whole rise is therefore one fourth the run of the middle jack rafter, or one eighth the square width of the building, or 4 feet 4.05 inches, the square of which is 2,709.2025 inches. The run of the hip rafter we have already proved to be equal to the side of the building, or 20 feet=240 inches, the square of which is 57,600 inches. The square root of the sum of the above two numbers is 245.56 inches, or 20 feet 5.56 inches, which is the length of the hip rafter.

In a similar manner the length of the *middle jack rafters* is found to be 17 feet 10.26 inches. The length of the shortest jack rafters is obtained in the same manner as in hip roofs generally.

The *bevels of the hip jack rafters* are obtained by the same rule as in octagonal roofs.

The *backing of the hip rafters* is found on the square by taking $\frac{7}{12}$ of its rise on the tongue, and its length on the blade.

Plate 21.

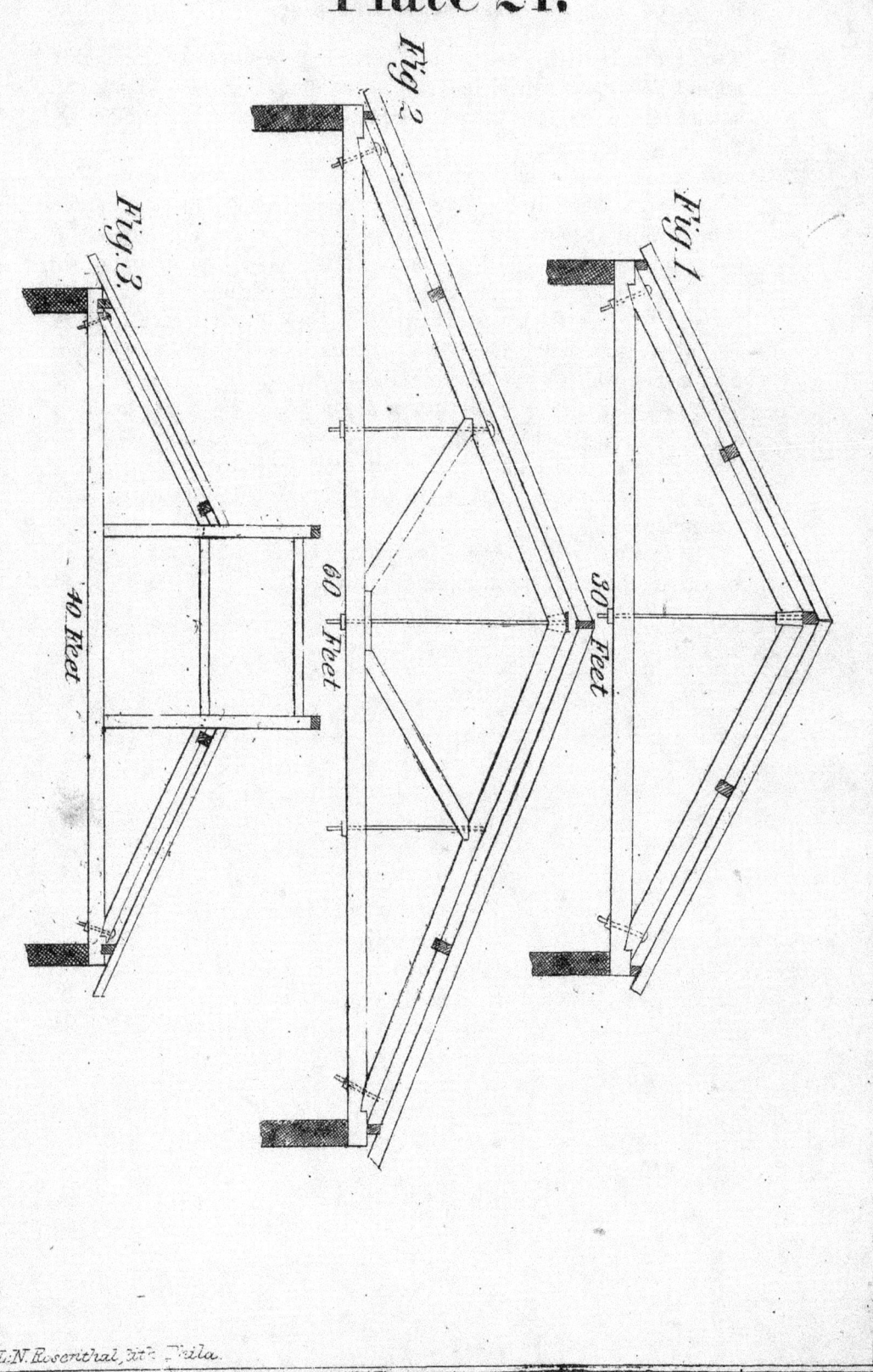

PLATE 21.

ROOFS OF BRICK AND STONE BUILDINGS.

Plate 21, Fig. 1, exhibits a simple and excellent mode of framing a roof of a moderate span of from 25 to 35 feet, designed for a stone or brick building. The iron bolts, by which the feet of the principal rafters are secured to the tie-beam, are $\frac{3}{4}$ of an inch in diameter, and the supporting rod in the middle is 1 inch in diameter. The block between the upper ends of the principal rafters, is beveled to suit the pitch of the roof, while the ends of the principal rafters are square. The block should be of hard wood, and placed with its grain running in the same direction as that of the rafters, to avoid shrinkage.

By means of the supporting rods, any proper degree of camber or crowning can be given to the tie-beam.

The bolts and rods in this and the following figures are left rough in the Plates, to show them more distinctly; but if the rooms beneath are to be ceiled or plastered, the heads of the bolts should be countersunk into the beam, and the nuts screwed upon the upper ends.

Fig. 2 represents another style of roof, with two braces and two additional rods to each bent, and also a 2 inch block of hard wood about 2 feet long, placed between the feet of the braces. The grain of this block should also run parallel with the beam.

Length and Bevels of the Braces.

Suppose the distance of the upper end of the brace mortice in the principal rafter from the heel of that rafter to be five ninths of the whole length of that rafter, then the perpendicular let fall from the heel of the brace to the tie-beam will be five ninths of the rise of the rafter—and this we will call the *rise of the brace;* then also the distance from the foot of this perpendicular to the toe of the foot of the brace, will be four ninths of one half the length of the tie-beam less 2 feet— one foot for the setting back of the principal rafter, and one foot for half the block at the foot of the brace: this is the *run of the brace;* then the sum of the squares of the rise and the run will give the square of the length of the brace, the square root of which will be that length from the lower toe to the upper heel.

The Span of this Roof

May be from 50 to 65 feet. The middle rod should be $1\frac{1}{4}$ inches, the others $\frac{3}{4}$ of an inch.

Dimensions of Timbers for Figs. 1 & 2.

For both frames—Rafters, 2 by 6; plates and purlin plates, 6 by 8.
For each bent in Fig. 1—Tie-beams, 8 by 10; principal rafters, 7 by 9.
For each bent in Fig. 2—Tie-beams, 10 by 12; principal rafters, 7 by 10; braces, 6 by 7.

The bents in each frame may be from 10 to 14 feet apart.

Fig. 3 represents a simple mode of framing a roof for a shop or foundry where it is required to have a ventilator.

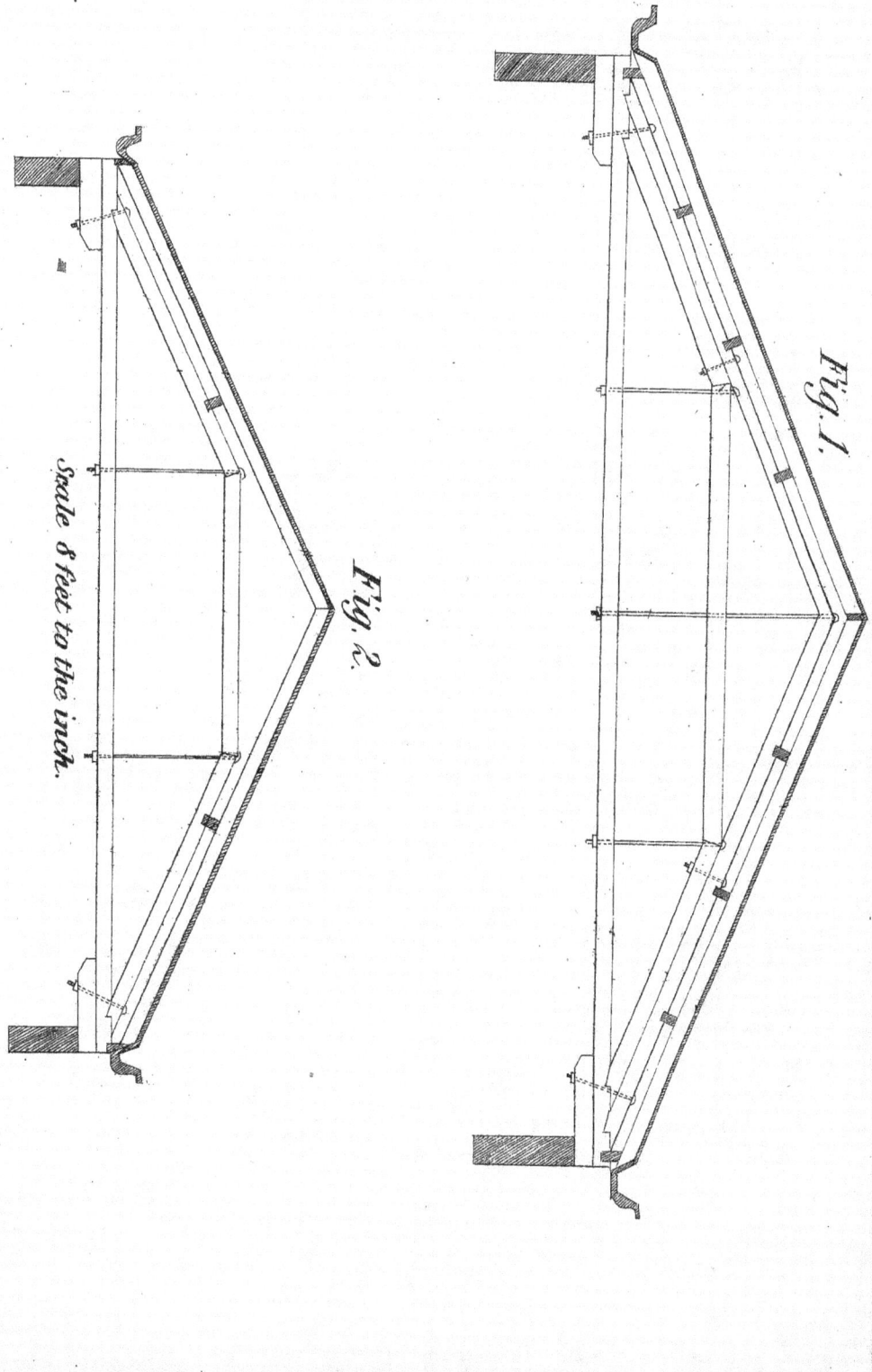

PLATE 22.

Fig. 1 represents a bent of a very strong roof, designed for machine shops and other buildings, where it is necessary for great weights or heavy machinery to be supported by them. The Author of this work has superintended the construction of roofs of this kind upon the machine shops for the Railroad Works at Peoria, Ill., and at Davenport, Iowa, where they have proved sufficiently strong to sustain locomotive engines weighing more than twenty tons, when hoisted from the ground, and suspended by chains from the roof for repairs.

The width of the building represented in Fig. 1 is 50 feet; the principal rafter is set back a foot from the end of the tie-beam, to give room for the wall plate; the rise of the roof is 5 inches to the foot. In framing roofs of this kind, the supporting rods should be furnished before commencing the frame: for then the length of the short principal rafters and that of the straining beam, can be regulated or pro portioned according to the length of the rods. It is best, however, for the middle rod to be twice the length of the short ones, reckoning from the upper surface of the beam to the upper surface of the principal rafters, and allowing 1 foot more to each rod for the thickness of the beam, and the nut and washer. For example, the middle rod is 11 feet long, and the short ones 6 feet each; which, after allowing 1 foot, as above mentioned, makes the length of the long one, above the work side of the beam, twice that of the short ones.

The length of the rod above the beam is the rise of the rafter, and the distance from the centre of the rod to the foot of the rafter is the run of the rafter; the length of the rafter can therefore be found from the Common Rafter Table.

Length of the Straining Beam.

Add the run of the short principal rafter to the lower end bevel of the long one; subtract this sum from the run of the long principal, and the difference will be half the length of the straining beam.

The *bolsters* under the ends of the tie beams are of the same thickness as that, and about 5 feet long.

Fig. 2 is in every respect similar to Fig. 1, with the exception of the long principal rafters and the middle supporting rod being omitted. This roof is suitable for blacksmith shops and foundries, as it is also capable of sustaining great weights, and may be very convenient for the safe storing of unwrought iron bars upon the beams.

PLATE 23.

This plate exhibits sections of three roofs, of different dimensions, but similar to each other in style. This style is ancient, and, no doubt, has been proved of sufficient strength; but it is not recommended for convenience or economy, except where labor is cheap, timber plentiful, and iron scarce.

In Fig. 1, the post in the middle is called the *king post*, and the other two *queen posts*. The tie beam is secured to their feet by iron straps; and braces extend in pairs from the posts to the principal rafters, as represented in the Plate. The heads of the posts are beveled to correspond with the pitch of the roof, and the ends of the principal rafters are left square.

The manner of scarfing the tie beam is represented immediately below.

Fig. 2 is very similar in design to Fig. 1, in the preceding Plate, the principal difference consisting in having king and queen posts instead of supporting rods.

Fig. 3 shows the ridge pole supported by braces from the ends of the straining beam. The king post is, therefore, omitted; and the space between the queen posts may be appropriated for an attic chamber. The queen posts are let into the tie-beam an inch or more, to prevent displacement by the lateral pressure of the braces.

Plate 23.

Fig. 1.

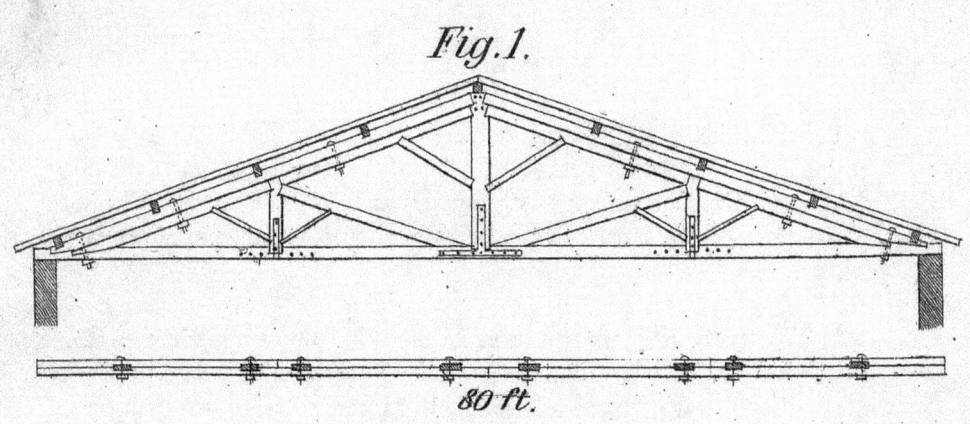

80 ft.

Fig. 2.

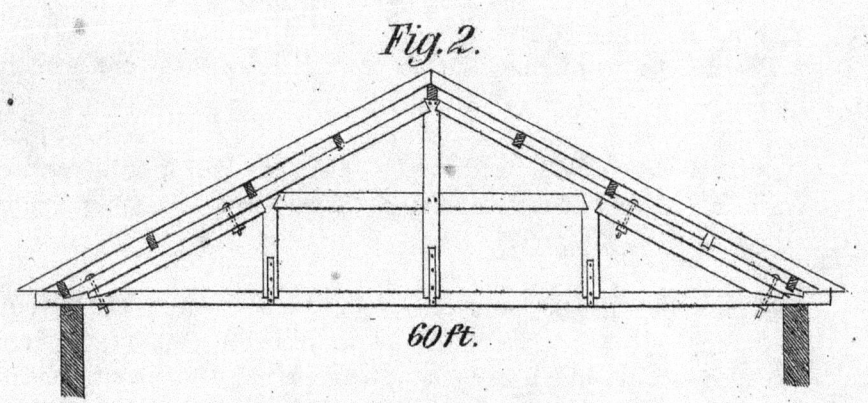

60 ft.

Fig. 3.

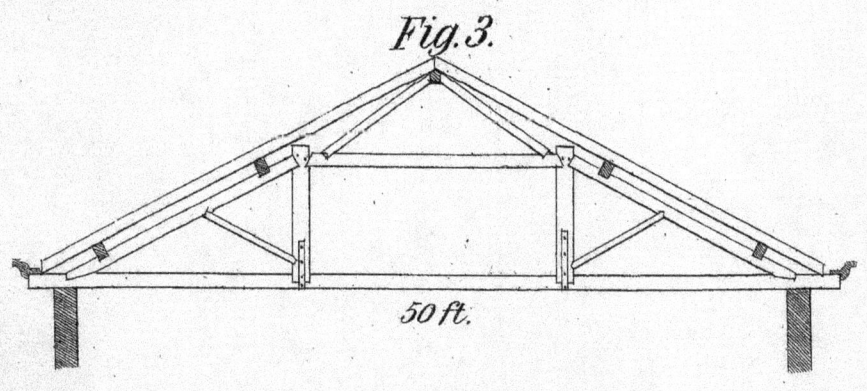

50 ft.

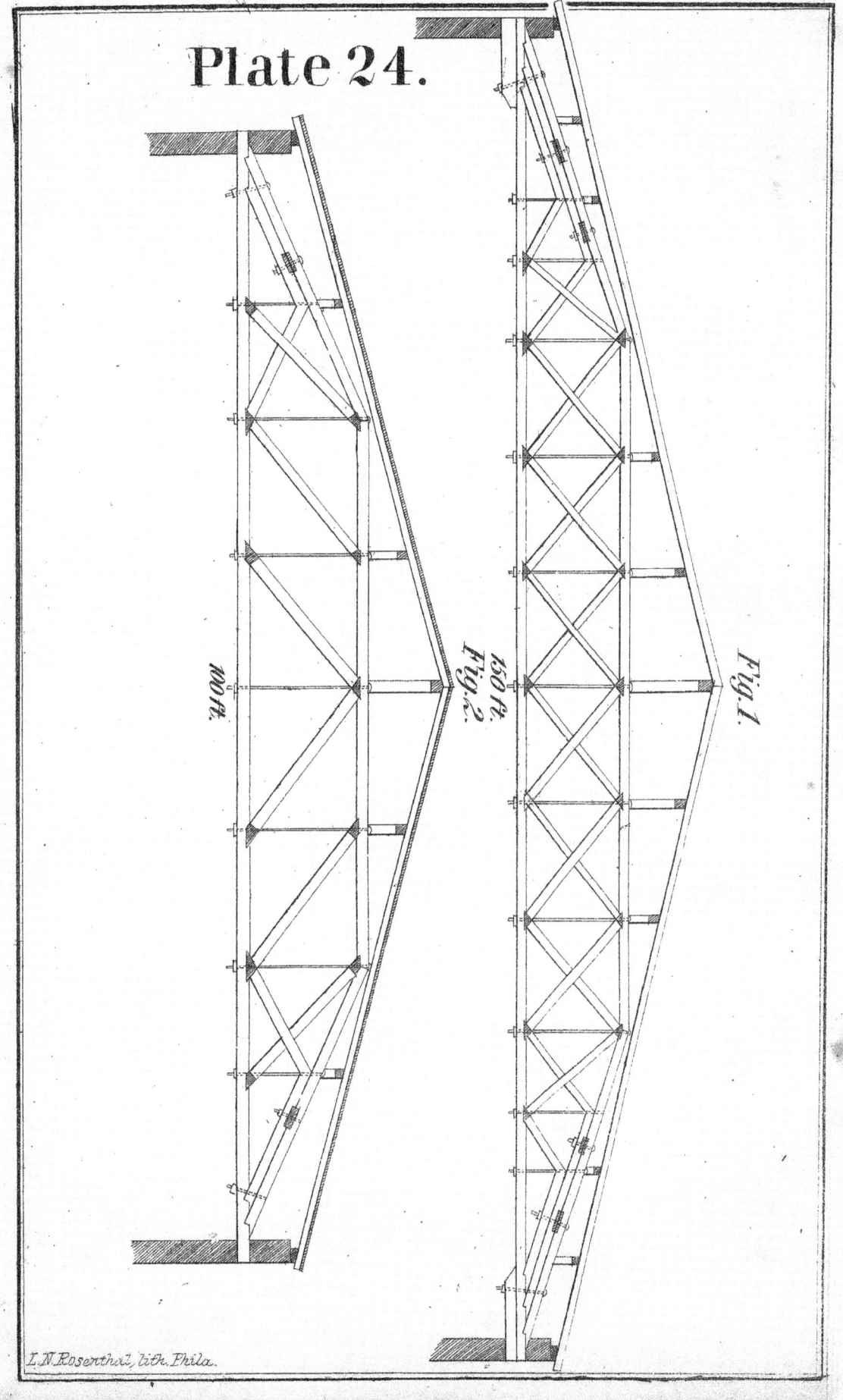

PLATE 24.

Plate 24 exhibits several designs for roofs in a new and improved style, particularly adapted to those of a great span, as they may be safely extended to a very considerable width, with less increase of weight, and less proportionate expense, than any of the older styles. The principle on which they are constructed is essentially the same as that of the Howe Bridge. The braces are square at the ends, the hard wood blocks between them being beveled and placed as described in the foregoing Plates. Each truss of this frame supports a purlin post and plate, as represented.

These roofs are easily made nearly flat, and thereby adapted to metallic covering, by carrying the walls above the tie beams to any desired height, without altering the pitch of the principal rafters, which ought to have a rise of at least 4 inches to the foot, to give a sufficient brace to the upper chord or straining beam.

Fig. 1 is represented with counter-braces; and

Fig. 2 without them. The counter-braces do not add any thing to the mere support of the roof, and are entirely unnecessary in frames of churches, or other public buildings, where there is no jar; but they may very properly be used in mill frames, or other buildings designed for heavy machinery.

PLATE 25.

This Plate exhibits two plans for roofs of the same style as the last, but of simpler construction, and designed for a shorter span.

In Fig. 2 the middle truss is omitted, to afford room for an attic chamber.

Plate 25.

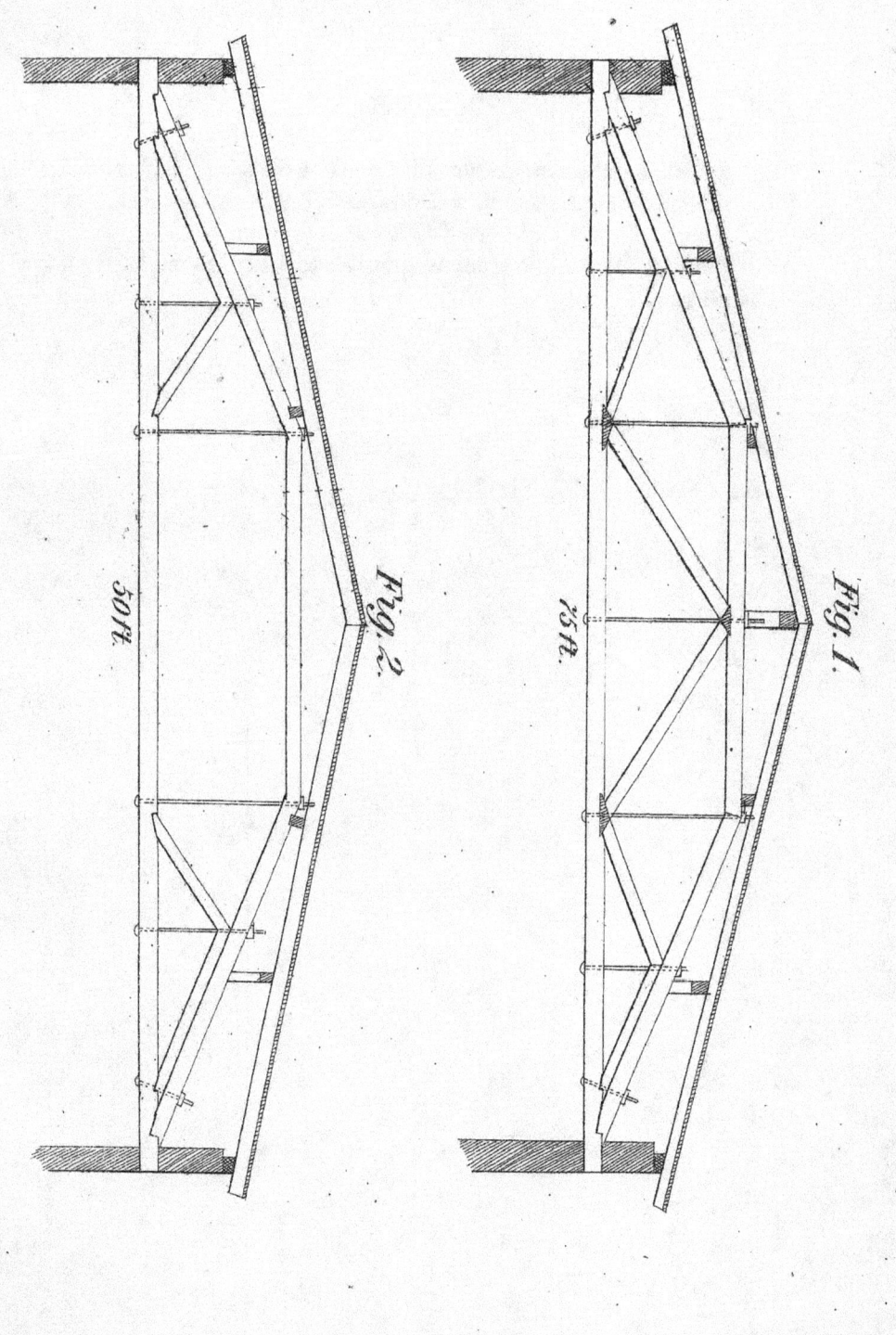

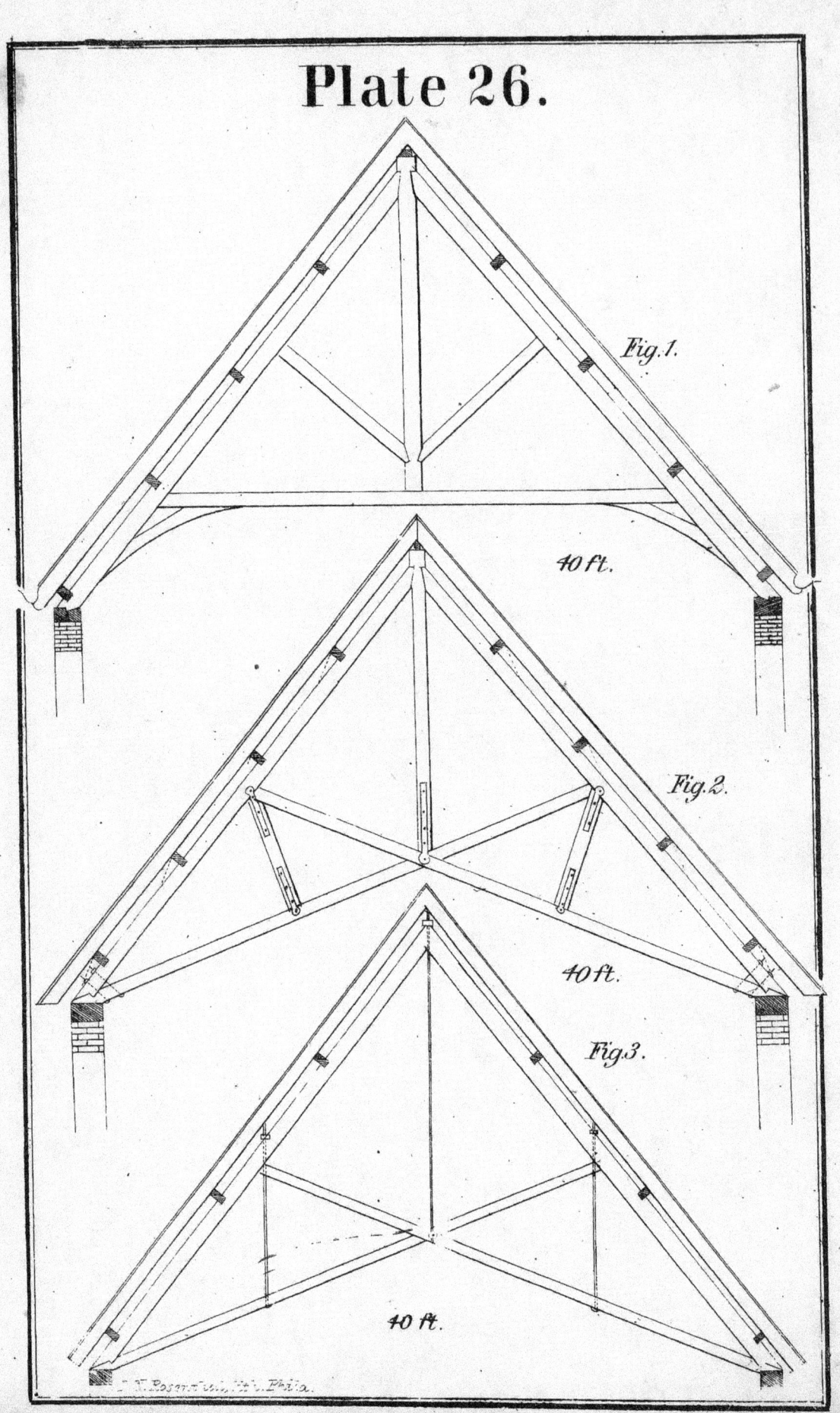

PLATE 26.

This Plate exhibits several designs of Gothic roofs, the manner of framing which is sufficiently indicated by the Plate.

Fig. 1 is constructed entirely of wood.

Fig. 2 of wood, strengthened with iron straps and bolts; and

Fig. 3 with still less wood, but supported by iron rods; and, undoubtedly, the strongest roof of the three.

The first is, however, a neat, cheap, and very simple plan, and sufficiently strong for a roof having a steep pitch, and of not more than 40 feet span.

PLATE 27.

Plate 27 represents two designs for church roofs, with arched or vaulted naves.

In Fig. 1 the arch is formed of 2 inch planks, from 6 to 8 inches wide, after being wrought into the proper curve. These planks are doubled, so as to break joints, and firmly spiked together. Lighter arches, of similar construction, are sprung, at a distance of 16 inches apart, between the bents, for supporting the lathing.

In Fig. 2 the arch is formed of 3 inch planks, 10 to 12 inches wide, and made in three sections, and spiked to the braces, as represented.

Note.—The foregoing designs for roofs have been selected from more than a hundred drafts in the Author's possession, and are believed to be the best selection ever offered to the public eye. The number could have been increased with ease to an indefinite extent; but it has been deemed necessary to insert those only which are at once excellent and practicable, and which combine the latest improvements.

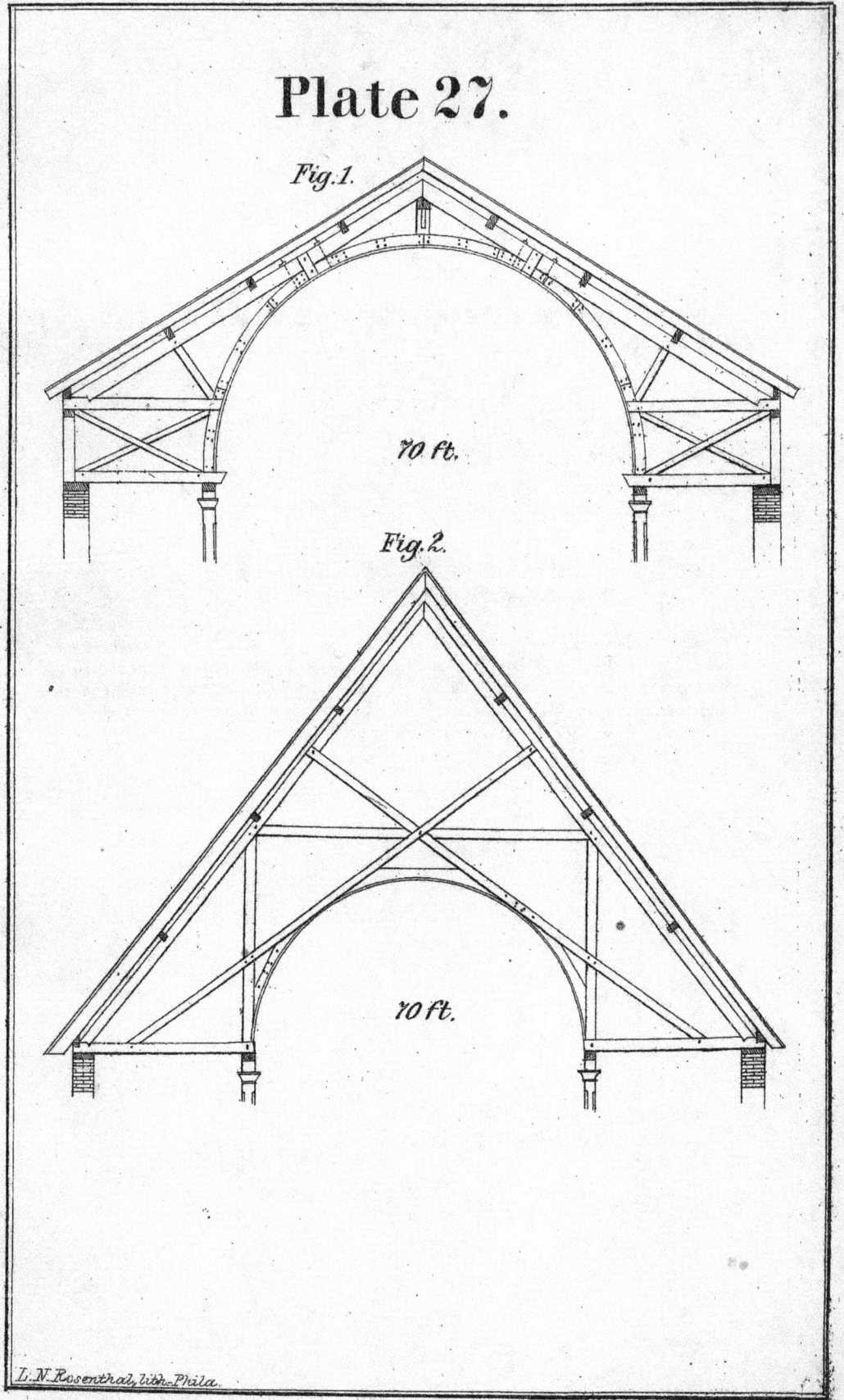

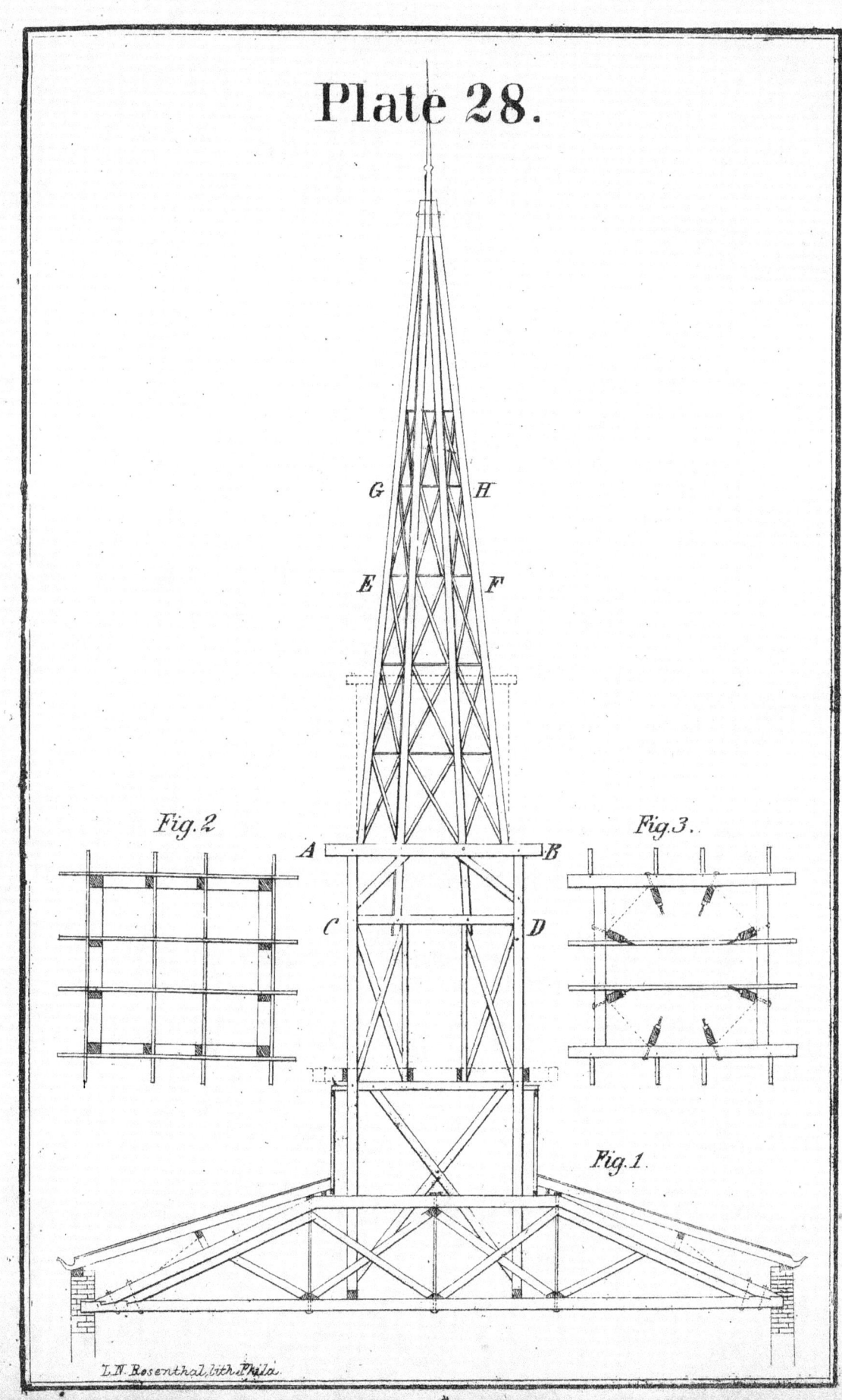

PLATE 28.

Plate 28 exhibits the frame-work of a church spire, 85 feet high above the tie beam, or cross timber of the roof. This is framed square as far as the top of the second section, above which it is octagonal. It will be found most convenient to frame and raise the square portion first; then to frame the octagonal portion, or spire proper, before raising it: in the first place letting the feet of the 8 hip rafters of the spire, each of which is 48 feet long, rest upon the tie beam and joists of the main building. The top of the spire can, in that situation, be conveniently finished and painted, after which it may be raised half way to its place, when the lower portion can be finished as far down as the top of the third section. The spire should then be raised and bolted to its place, by bolts at the top of the second section at AB, and also at the feet of the hip rafters at CD. The third section can then be built around the base of the spire proper; or the spire can be finished, as such, to the top of the second section, dispensing with the third, just as the taste or ability of the parties shall determine.

Fig. 2 presents a horizontal view of the top of the first section.

Fig. 3 is a horizontal view of the top of the second section, after the spire is bolted to its place.

The lateral braces in the spire are halved together, at their intersection with each other, and beveled and spiked to the hip rafters at the ends. These braces may be dispensed with on a low spire.

A conical finish can be given to the spire above the sections, by making the outside edges of the cross timbers circular.

The bevels of the hip rafters are obtained in the usual manner for octagonal roofs, as described in Plate 20

Note.—In most cases the *side* of an octagon is given as the basis of calculation in finding the width and other dimensions; but in spires like this, where the lower portion is square, we are required to find the side from a given width. The second section in this steeple, within which the octagonal spire is to be bolted, is supposed to be 12 feet square outside; and the posts being 8 inches square, the width of the octagon at the top of this section, as represented in Fig. 3, is 10 feet 8 inches, and its side is 4 feet 5.02 inches, as demonstrated in the explanation of the Table for Octagonal Roofs (No. 3).

The side of any other octagon may be found from this by proportion, since all regular octagons are similar figures, and their sides are to each other as their widths, and, conversely, their widths are to each other as their sides.—See Explanation of Table No. 3.

PLATE 29.

Plate 29 exhibits the plan of a large dome of 60 or 75 feet span, built upon a strong circular stone or brick wall. In constructing this roof, there are four bents framed, like the one exhibited in Fig. 1, all intersecting each other beneath the king post at the centre. The tie beams in the first and second bents are of full length, and halved together; those in the third and fourth bents are in half lengths, and mitred to the intersection of the first and second.

The King Post.

Has eight faces, and on each face two braces; one large brace from the top of the post to the end of the tie beam, and one small brace from the bottom of the post to the middle of the large brace. These four tie beams are supported by eight posts, extending from the top of the main wall to the ends of the beams, and each one braced as represented in the figure.

Two circular arches, constructed of planks, as described in Plate 27, are then sprung, one above and one below each bent, as represented in the figure. Between each of these four arches, three others are constructed, supported by short timbers, framed into the ties of the tie beam, as represented in Fig. 2.

Fig. 2 is a horizontal section of the dome, drawn through it at the main tie beam AB, which corresponds with AB, in Fig. 1.

Fig. 3 is a horizontal view of the apex of the dome, where all the 32 arches intersect each other, showing the mode of beveling them at their intersection.

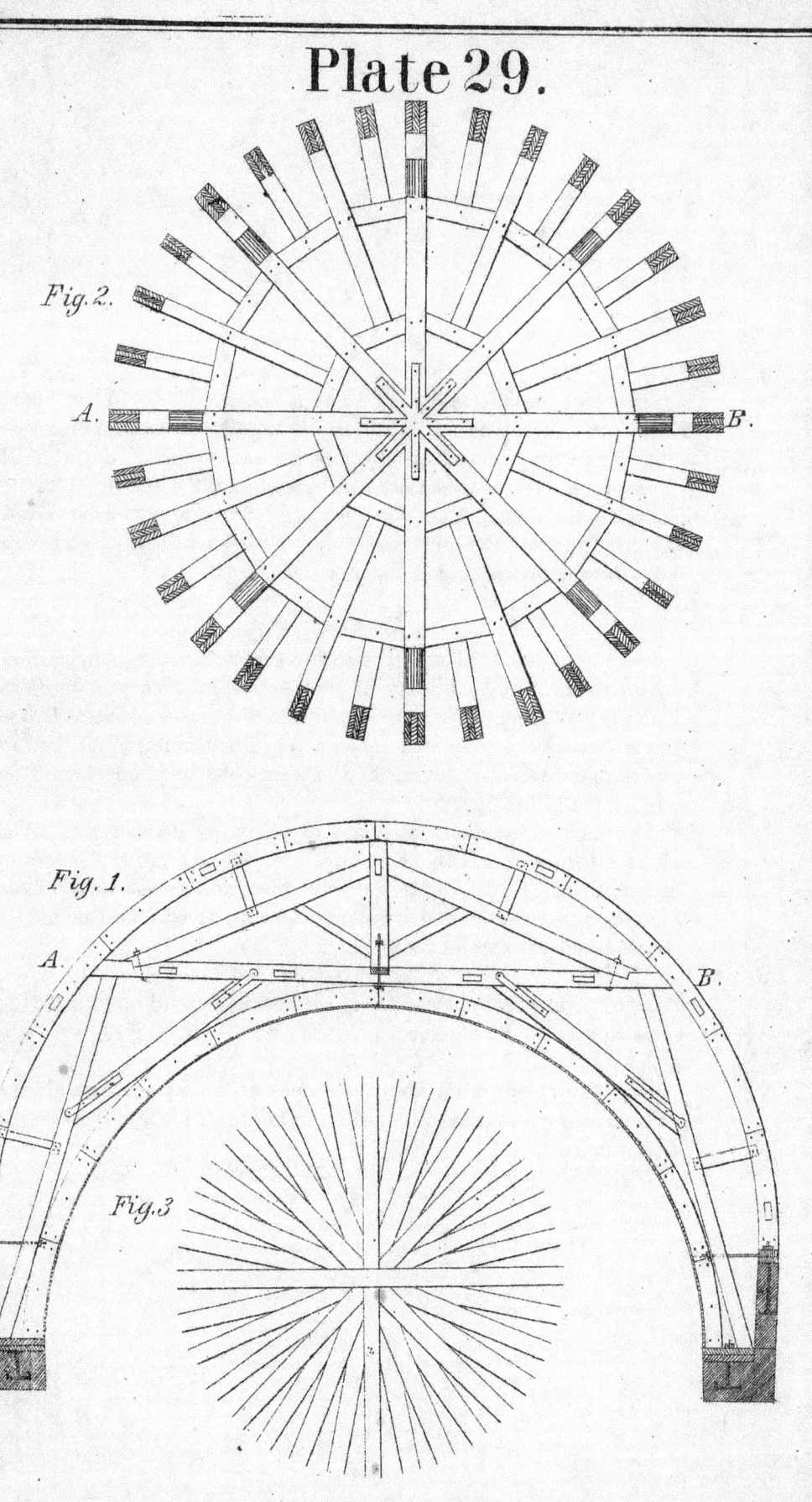

PART III.

Plate 30.

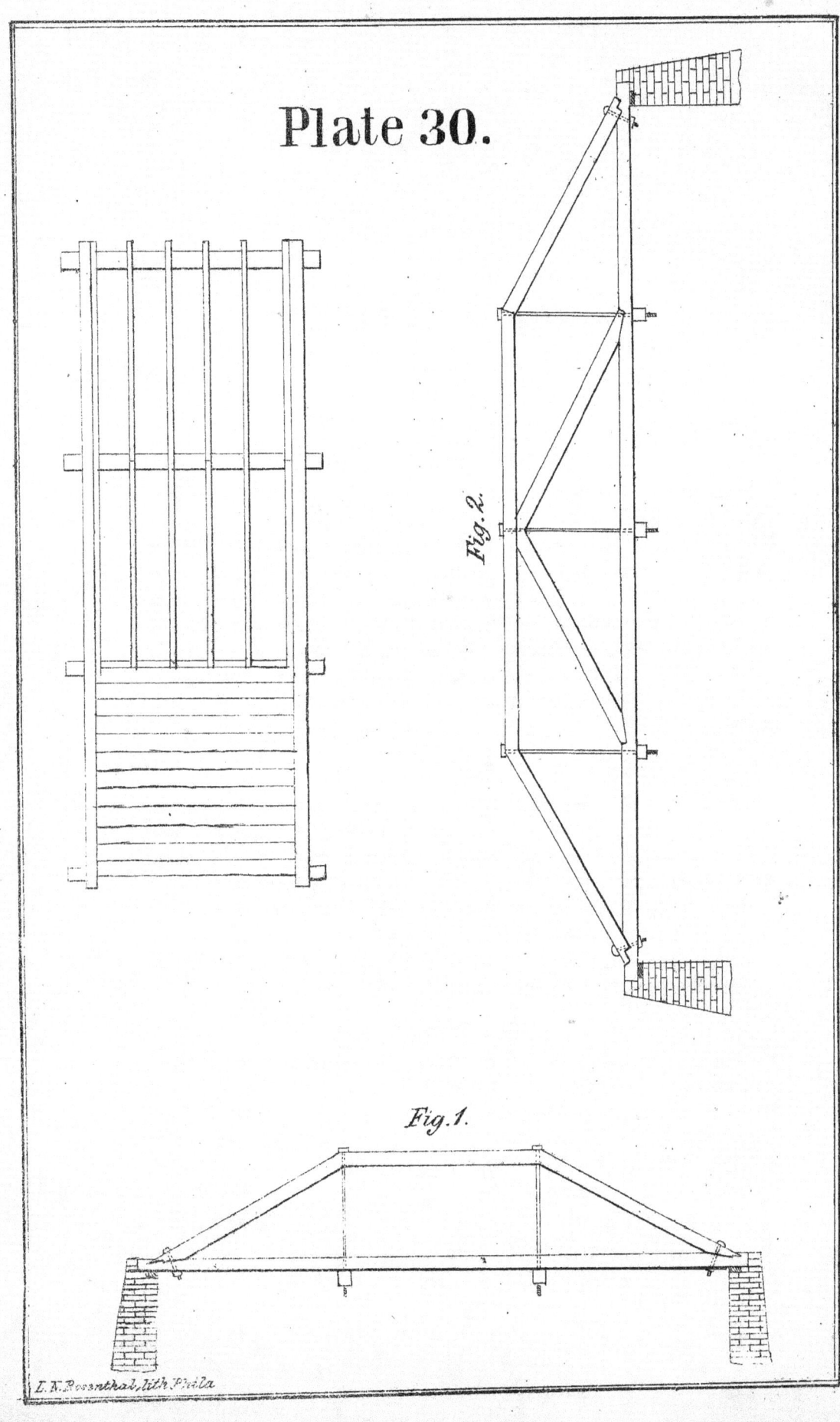

Fig. 1.

Fig. 2.

BRIDGE BUILDING.

PLATE 30.

STRAINING BEAM BRIDGES.

Plate 30, Fig. 1 represents a *straining beam bridge* of 30 feet span, designed for a common highway. The stringers or main timbers are 35 feet long, extending over each abutment to a distance of $2\frac{1}{2}$ feet. The straining beam is equal in length to $\frac{1}{3}$ of the span, or 10 feet. The supporting rods are 8 feet 2 inches long: 1 foot is allowed for the thickness of the stringer, 10 inches for the needle beam, and 4 inches nut head and washers; leaving 6 feet as the rise of the brace, or the distance of the top of the straining beam from the top of the stringer.

The *length of the brace* can therefore be found, as usual, by extracting the square root of the sum of the squares of the run and the rise.

Bevels.

The bevel at the foot of the brace is like that at the foot of a rafter, and is obtained in the same manner. The bevel at the upper end of the brace and the bevel of the straining beam are equal to each other, and are each equal to half that of a rafter of the same rise and run.

Fig. 2 exhibits the horizontal plan of the floor timbers, and the manner of laying both the joists and the planks.

A moderate degree of camber should be given to every bridge of this kind, by screwing up the supporting rods.

Bill of Timber.

2 Stringers,	12 by 12, in. 35 feet long, Board measure	=840 feet.
4 Braces,	8 by 10, " 12 " " " "	=160 "
2 Straining beams	8 by 10, " 10 " " " "	=133 "
2 Wall plates,	10 by 12, " 16 " " " "	=320 "
2 Needle beams,	8 by 10, " 18 " " " "	=240 "
5 Joists,	3 by 10, " 12 " " " "	=150 "

5 Joists, 2 by 10, 22 feet long, Board measure=245 feet.
932 feet, 2-inch planks " " =932 "

Total timber, B. M. 3020 "

Bill of Iron.

4 Supporting rods, 1¼ in. diameter, 8 ft. 2 in. long, each 34½ lbs.=138 lbs.
8 Washers, 4 lbs. each; and 4 nuts 1 lb. each, = 36 "
4 Bolts, 1 in. diameter 22 in. long, each 5½ lbs. = 22 "
8 Washers, 1 lb. each, and 4 nuts ¾ lb. each, = 11 "
40 lbs. spikes, = 40 "

247 "

Estimate of Cost.

3020 feet lumber, @ $15 per M. =$45.30
247 lbs. iron, @ 7c. " lb. = 17.29
Workmanship, @ $10 " M. Board measure. = 30.20

Total cost, $92.79

Fig. 2. In respect to this bridge, it is only necessary to say that it is constructed upon the same principle as the former; the difference being caused only by the increase of the span, and this difference being sufficiently represented by the Plate.

In raising the former of these bridges, no false work or temporary supports are needed, but for this one they may be.

Concerning the economy and durability of these bridges, it may be proper to observe that they are comparatively simple and cheap; and they are also sufficiently strong, so long as the supports maintain their vertical position. But this plan has two objections.

1. The absence of side braces induces a *leaning* or twisting of the braces, caused by their pressure toward each other; and when this *twisting*, or *torsion* as it is often called, has once commenced, it cannot well be remedied. It may, however, be guarded against, to a certain extent, by such a modification of the design as will allow of two supporting rods at each end of the needle beams—these rods being crossed; one passing inside of the stringer, and the other at some distance outside of it, toward the end of the needle beam.

2. The absence of counter braces exposes the bridge to injury from vibration; which is specially destructive to the stone-work of the abutments, the repeated jars being almost sure to break the mortar and loosen the stones. The use of a wall-plate serves in some degree to obviate this objection; and in case of the bridge being supported by trestles, it disappears.

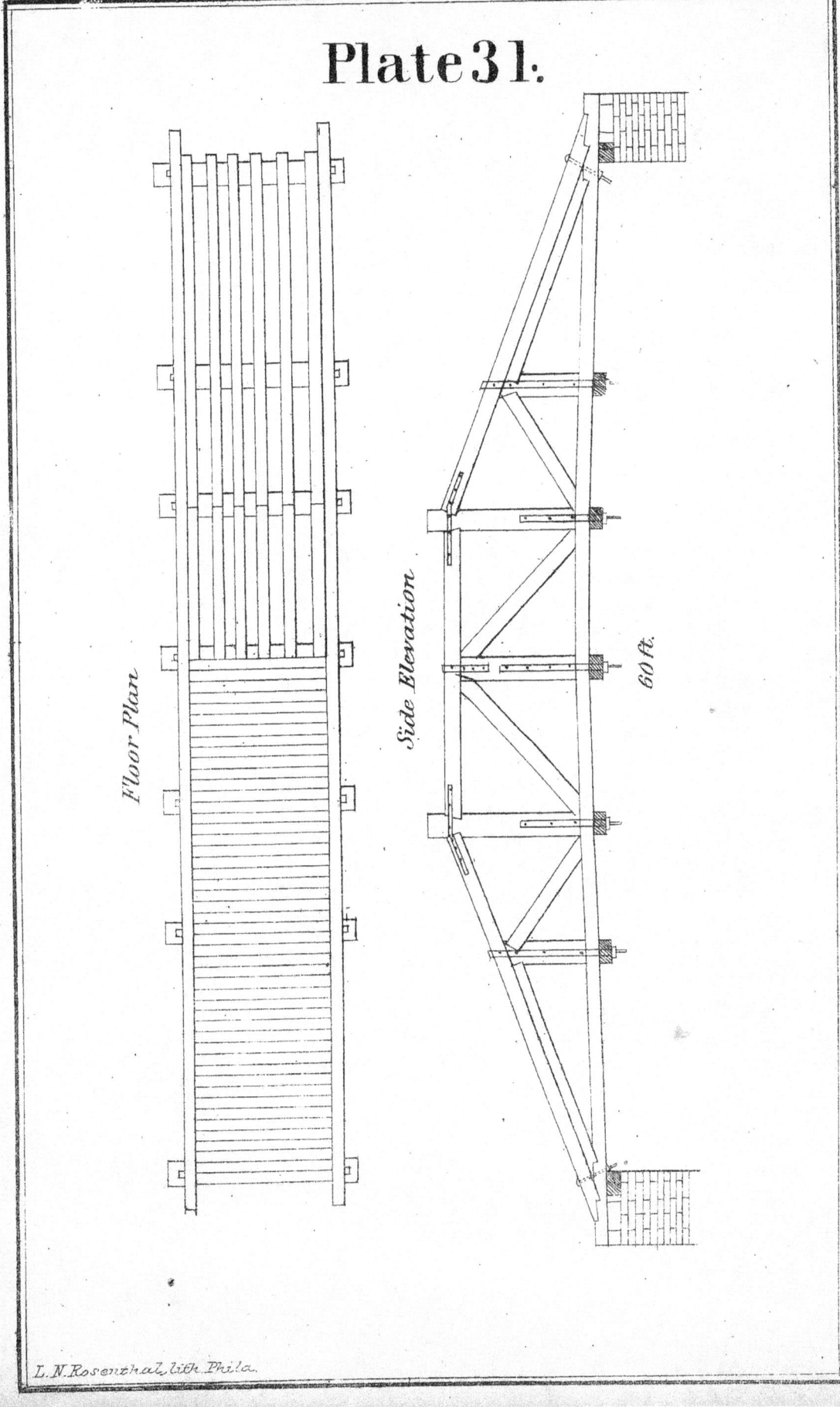

PLATE 31.

This bridge is more expensive and more durable than those before represented, as it is also less liable to the objections mentioned concerning them. The counter braces of this bridge are sufficient to prevent injurious effects from vibrations; and the size of the posts, or upright ties, when secured by straps of iron, as represented, will also prevent the torsion or twisting of the braces, to which the others are liable. The manner of framing this bridge is sufficiently indicated by the Plate; and the lengths and bevels of the braces are obtained as usual.

Bill of Timber.

2 String pieces,	12 by 12 in. 65 feet long	1560 feet
2 Straining beams,	12 by 12 " 18 " "	432 "
4 Long braces,	12 by 12 " 26 " "	1248 "
4 Short end braces,	10 by 12 " 15 " "	600 "
4 Middle braces,	10 by 12 " 10 " "	400 "
4 Counter braces,	10 by 12 " 9 " "	360 "
4 Long posts,	12 by 12 " 10 " "	480 "
2 Middle posts,	12 by 12 " 9 " "	216 "
4 Short posts,	12 by 12 " 6 " "	288 "
2 Wall plates,	6 by 12 " 18 " "	216 "
5 Needle beams,	10 by 10 " 20 " "	833 "
12 Joists,	3 by 10 " 24 " "	720 "
6 Joists,	3 by 10 " 18 " "	270 "
2000 feet, B. M., of floor plank,	16 " "	2000 "
		9623 "

PLATE 32.

This Plate presents a view of a bridge offered as an improvement of the Howe Bridge, of a moderate span, by shortening the upper chord, and bracing the ends of it in the same manner as in a straining beam bridge. In the Howe Bridge, the upper chord is of the same length as the lower one, and the braces and counter braces are placed in a uniform manner throughout the entire length. In the plan represented in this Plate, by reducing the length of the upper chord to the limit of a single piece of timber, it is proposed to secure, at least, an equal degree of strength to the ordinary Howe Bridge, and at the same time to effect economy in both material and labor.

The ends of the braces are left square, and the proper bevels are made upon the angle blocks, which are of hard wood or of cast iron, and are let into the chords to the depth of 1 inch or more.

The main braces all lean inward toward the centre of the span, and are double, passing one outside and one inside of the counter braces, which are single, leaning in the opposite direction from the centre toward the ends, each brace passing between each pair of main braces, and are all three bolted together at their intersection.

The lower chords in each truss, or each side, are three in number, and bolted together in the most firm manner possible. Hard wood keys, 2 inches thick, 6 inches wide, and 12 inches long, are inserted on each side of every joint, and at certain intervals even where there are no joints. These keys are let into the chords only about three fourths of an inch on each side, leaving a half inch space between the chords for the free circulation of air.

Bill of Timber.

2 Upper chord pieces,	10 by 14 in. 54 feet long	=1260 feet.
4 Long end braces,	10 by 14 " 22 " "	=1027 "
4 Short " "	6 by 6 " 12 " "	= 144 "
4 Short end counter braces,	4 by 6 " 12 " "	= 96 "
32 Middle main braces,	5 by 7 " 13 " "	=1212 "
12 Counter braces,	4 by 7 " 13 " "	= 364 "
6 Lower chord pieces,	6 by 12 " 31 " "	=1116 "
4 " " "	6 by 12 " 40 " "	= 960 "

Plate 32.

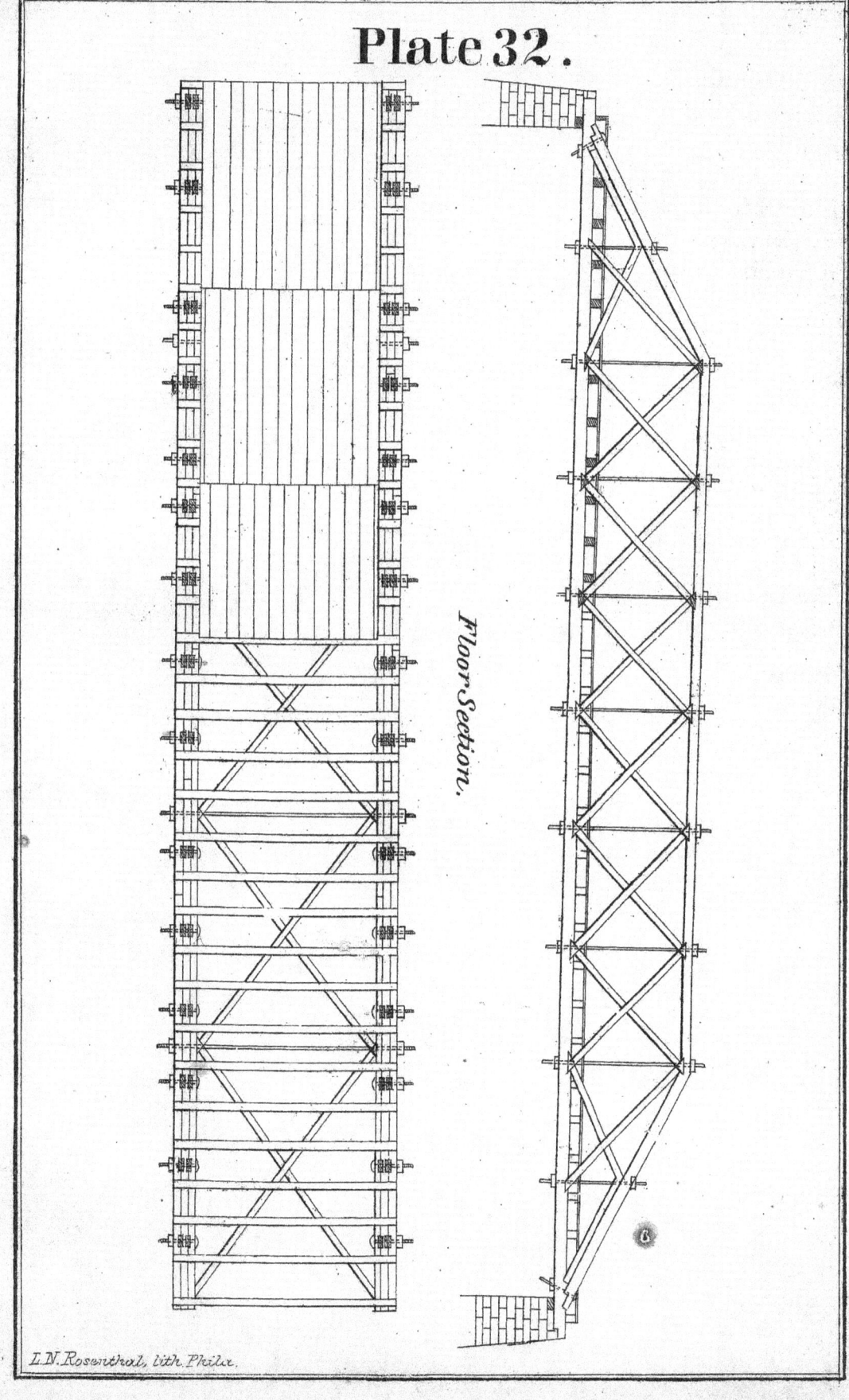

Floor Section.

4 Lower chord pieces,   6 by 12 in. 30 feet long = 720 feet.
4   "   "   "   12 by 2 " 23 "   "   = 552 "
2 Wall plates,   8 by 12 " 20 "   "   = 320 "
32 Joists,   4 by 12 " 18 "   "   =2304 "
10 Lateral braces,   4 by 6 " 24 "   "   = 480 "
3000 feet, B. M., floor plank,   3000 "

Bill of Iron

4 Middle support. rods, 1 in. diam., 12 ft. 2 in. long, 32 lbs. = 128 lbs.
8 Next to middle   " $1\frac{1}{4}$ "   12 " 2 "   "   51 " = 408 "
16 End rods, $1\frac{1}{2}$ "   12 " 2 "   "   73 " =1168 "
8 Short end rods, $1\frac{1}{2}$ "   6 " 1 "   " $36\frac{1}{2}$ " = 292 "
4 Long cross rods,   1   "   18 " 3 "   " $48\frac{1}{8}$ " = 194 "
4 End bolts,   1   "   2 " 0 "   " $5\frac{1}{4}$ " = 21 "
24 Lower chord bolts,   1   "   22 "   "   5   " = 120 "
16 Brace bolts, $\frac{3}{4}$ "   16 "   "   2   " = 32 "
72 Nuts for supporting rods,   2   " = 144 "
18 Plates "   "   " $\frac{3}{4}$ in. thick, 4 w., 14 long, 12 " = 216 "
18   "   "   "   "   "   4 w., 19 long, 16 " = 288 "
96 Washers,   1   " = 96 "
48 Nuts for small bolts,   1   " = 48 "

Note.—The cost of labor in constructing this bridge is estimated at $11.00 per thousand, B. M., of the timber required.

PLATE 33.

TRESTLE BRIDGES.

This Plate exhibits the design of a bridge supported from below; and, for a moderate span, it is one in which the important elements of simplicity, strength, and durability, are well combined.

The plan of this bridge is so simple, as to require little further explanation than the inspection of the Plate. It will be perceived that the bearings are 10 feet apart, and that the braces are framed to correspond. The cross timbers are extended out several feet on each side, to give room for bracing the hand-rail.

This bridge is supported by trestles; and the Plate represents the manner of framing the end ones and the middle one. It is of the utmost importance that the embankments behind the end trestles are perfectly solid, as on their firmness depends the whole strength of the bridge.

Bill of Timber for One Span.

4 String pieces,	12 by 12 in.,	28 feet long,	=1344 feet.
2 Straining beams,	12 by 16 "	30 " "	= 960 "
4 Long braces,	10 by 10 "	24 " "	= 800 "
4 Short braces,	10 by 10 "	14 " "	= 467 "
6 Cross timbers,	6 by 12 "	24 " "	= 864 "
12 Hand-rail posts,	6 by 6 "	4½ " "	= 162 "
104 feet (lineal) hand railing,	6 by 6 "		= 312 ".
12 Hand-rail braces,	3 by 4 "	4½ " "	= 54 "
12 Joists,	3 by 10 "	20 " "	= 600 "
6 "	3 by 10 "	11 " "	= 165 "
1660 feet, B. M., floor plank,			=1660 "
Total			7388 "

Bill of Timber for the Two End Trestles.

4 Posts,	12 by 12 in.,	13 feet long,	= 624 feet
8 Studs,	6 by 12 "	13 " "	= 624 "
4 "	6 by 12 "	8 " '	= 192 '

Plate 33.

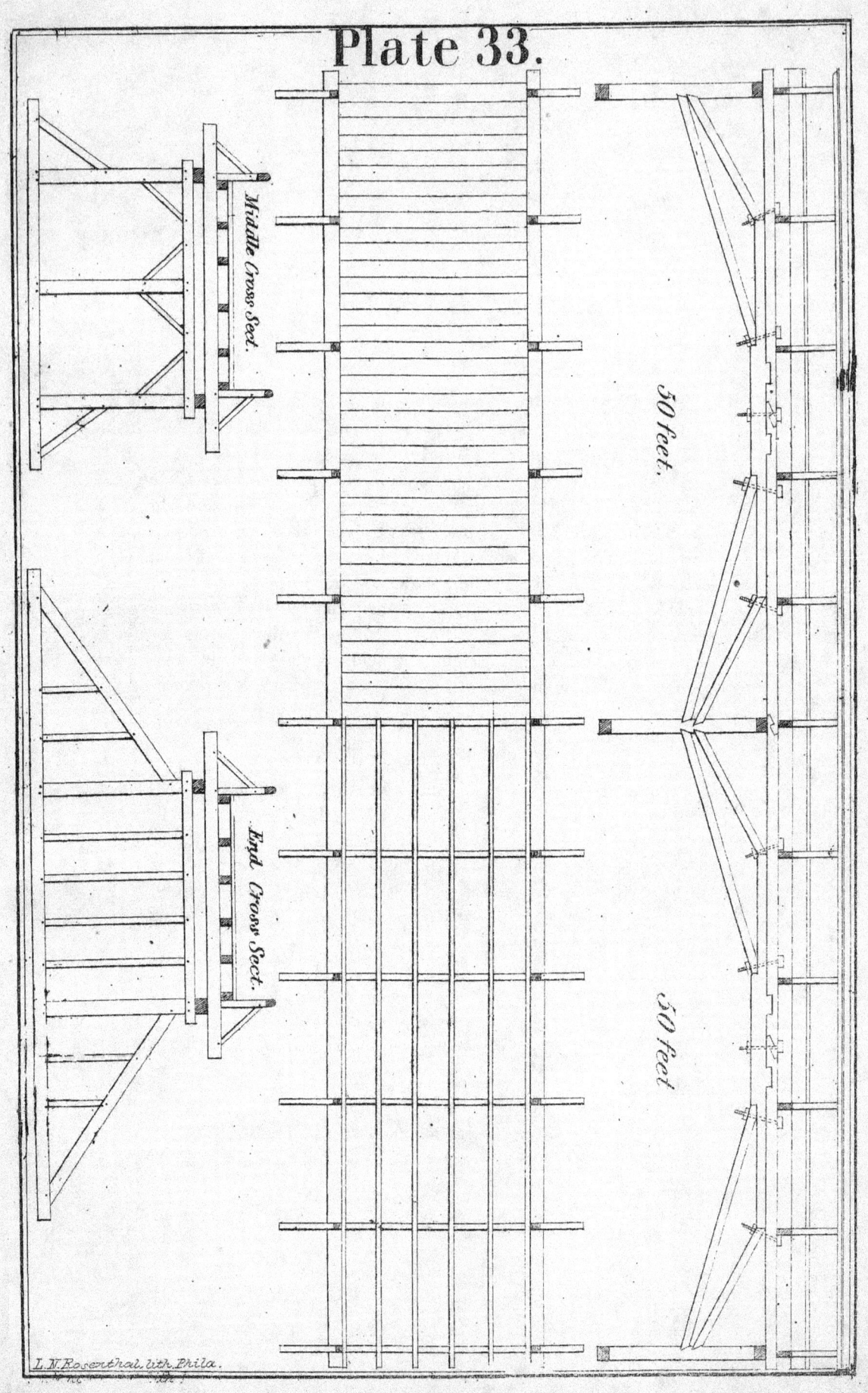

BRIDGE BUILDING. 99

4 Studs,	6 by 12 in., 6 feet long,	= 144 feet.
2 Mud sills,	12 by 12 " 52 " "	=1248 "
2 Caps,	12 by 12 " 20 " "	= 480 "
1000 ft., 2 in. hard wood plank for supporting embankm't,		=1000 "
		4312 "

Bill of Timber for Middle Trestle.

3 Posts,	12 by 12 in., 13 feet long, B.M.,	= 468 feet.
1 Mud sill,	12 by 12 " 30 " " "	= 360 "
1 Cap,	12 by 12 " 20 " " "	= 240 "
4 Post head braces,	4 by 4 " 5½ " " "	= 30 "
2 " foot braces,	8 by 8 " 8 " " "	= 90 "
		1188 "
For the two end trestles,		4312 "
Total of the three trestles, Board measure,		5500 "

PLATES 34 & 35.

Plates 34 and 35 represent a strong trestle bridge, such as is often used for rail-roads in crossing small streams and ravines, where the banks are high, and where there is little danger from ice. The Author of this work has constructed bridges of this kind at Spring Creek, Bureau Co., and at Nettle Creek, Grundy Co., on the Chicago and Rock Island Rail-road; and one on the plank road, between Peru and La Salle, in La Salle Co., Ill.—the last with posts, 51 feet high.

In *framing the trestles*, the posts are framed into the sills and caps as usual; but the braces are bolted upon the outside with inch bolts. The outside lower braces of the trestles, marked in the plan C, C, have 1 foot run to 2 feet rise; the posts of the trestles at A are set in such a manner as to act as braces, having 1 foot run to 4 feet rise. The *horizontal lateral braces* are also laid and bolted between the longitudinal timbers and cross timbers, without being framed into them. The lower longitudinal timbers are let into the posts to the depth of 2 inches, and lapped across the posts, one on one side, and the other on the other side, where they are bolted to the posts and to each other.

The *bearings are ten feet apart*, and each bearing is supported either by a post or a brace; these braces are framed to a 10 feet rise and a 9 feet run, and the upper ends are bolted to the longitudinal timbers, as represented in the Plate.

A *bill of timber and iron*, which is here subjoined, will assist the mechanic in framing a bridge of this kind more than any extended description could do. (The small letters in the Plate refer to the bolts.)

Bill of Timber.

6 Sills,	12 by 12 in.,	33 feet long, B. M.,	=2376 feet
1 Sill,	12 by 12 "	18 " " "	= 216 "
1 "	12 by 12 "	16 " " "	= 192 "
18 Posts,	12 by 12 "	25 " " "	=5400 "
3 "	12 by 12 "	12 " " "	= 432 "
3 "	12 by 12 "	10 " " "	= 360 "
6 Caps,	12 by 12 "	19 " " "	=1368 "
2 "	12 by 12 "	11 " " "	= 264 "
3 Lower cross timbers,	6 by 12 "	19 " " "	= 342 "

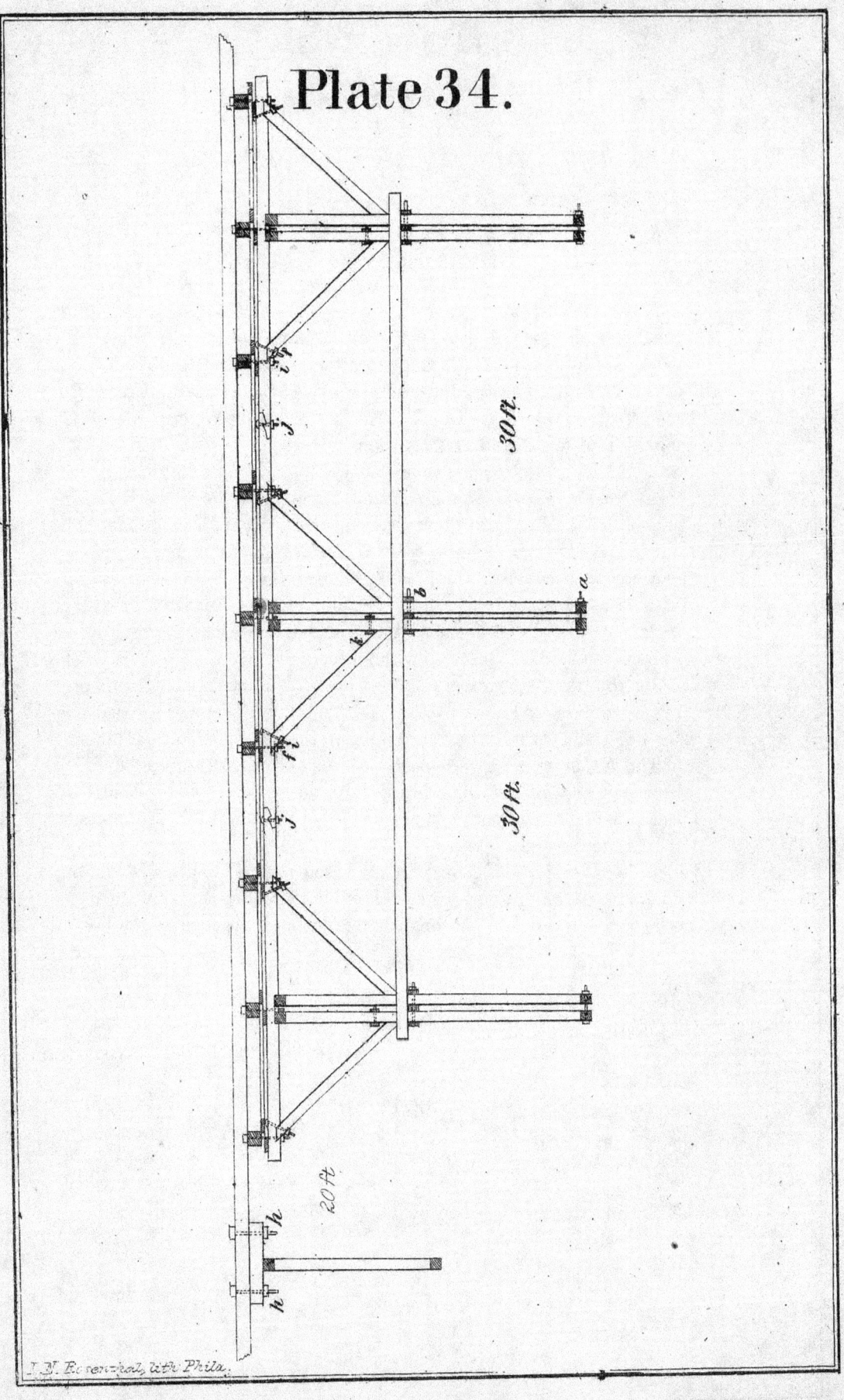

Plate 35.

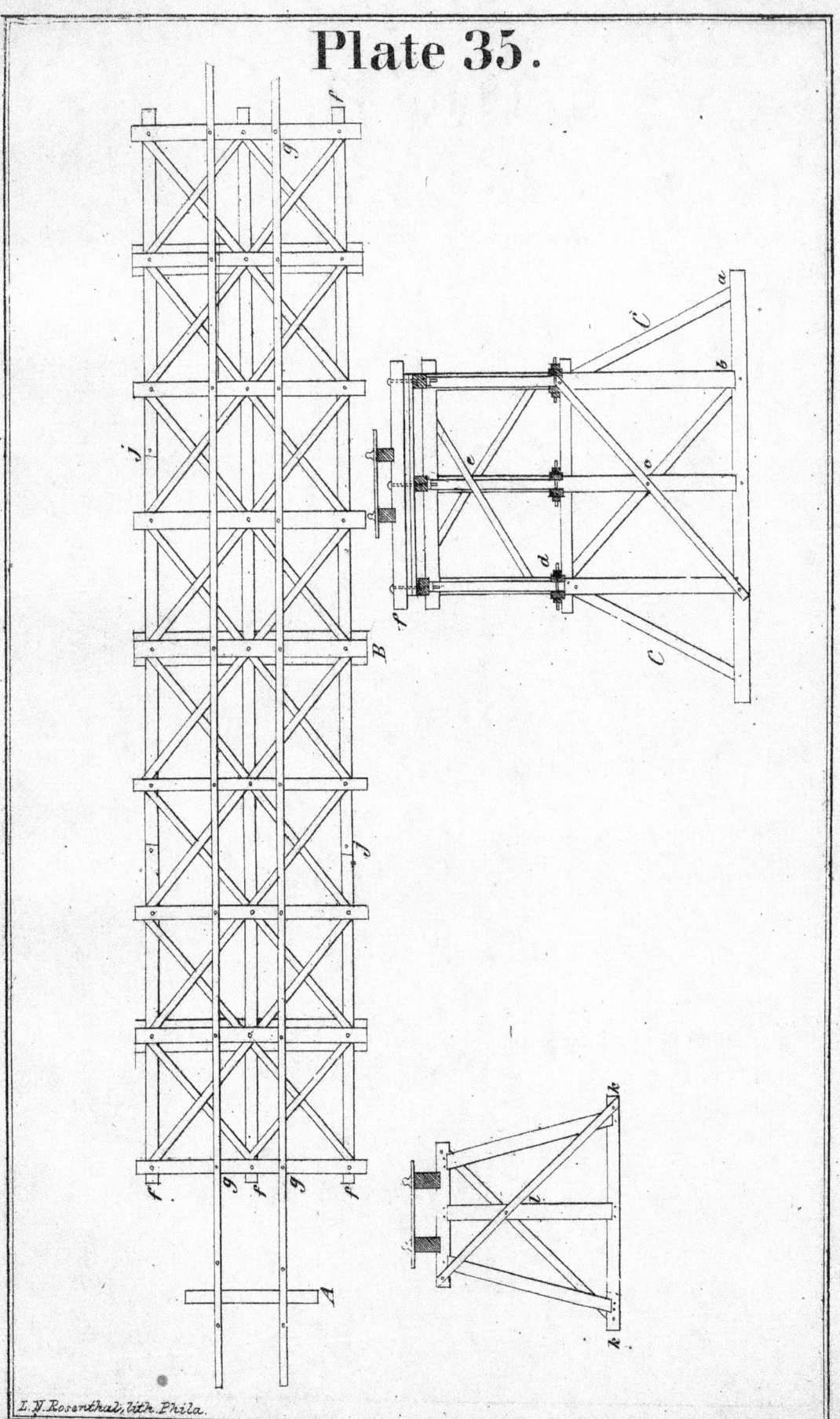

6 Lower longitudinal timbers,	6 by 12 in.,	35 feet long,	=1260 feet.
18 Braces,	8 by 10 "	14 " "	=1680 "
6 "	8 by 10 "	15 " "	= 600 "
6 String pieces,	9 by 12 "	27 " "	=1458 "
3 " "	9 by 12 "	32 " "	= 864 "
9 Cross timbers,	10 by 12 "	19 " "	=1710 "
16 Lateral braces,	4 by 8 "	27 " "	=1152 "
8 Rail stringers,	12 by 14 "	30 " "	=3360 "
4 Bolsters,	12 by 12 "	6 " "	= 288 "
6 Cross braces,	4 by 8 "	14 " "	= 224 "
6 " "	4 by 8 "	19 " "	= 304 "
2 " "	4 by 8 "	16 " "	= 85 "
2 " "	4 by 8 "	18 " "	= 96 "

Total, Board measure,   24,031 "

Bill of Iron.

6 Bolts (letter a),	32 in. long,	1 in. diam.,	= $42\frac{1}{2}$ lbs
12 " (" b),	36 "	" "	= $95\frac{1}{2}$ "
12 " (" c),	18 "	" "	= 24 "
18 " (" d),	22 "	" "	= $87\frac{1}{2}$ "
3 " (" e),	22 "	" "	= 15 "
27 " (" f),	31 "	" "	=185 "
18 " (" g),	26 "	" "	=$103\frac{1}{2}$ "
8 " (" h),	28 "	" "	= 50 "
294 Heads, nuts, and washers, @ 1 lb. each,			=294 "
18 Bolts (letter i),	20 in. long,	$\frac{3}{4}$ in. diam.,	= 45 "
6 " (" j),	11 "	" "	= $8\frac{1}{4}$ "
20 " (" k),	18 "	" "	= 45 "
2 " (" l),	22 "	" "	= $5\frac{1}{4}$ "
138 Bolt-heads, nuts, and washers, @ $\frac{3}{4}$ lb. each,			=103 "

Total of iron, $1100\frac{1}{2}$ "

PLATE 36.

ARCHED TRUSS BRIDGES.

This Plate represents a design of a Burr Bridge without counter braces, but combined with an *arch beam*. This mode of construction is designed either for railroad bridges, or for common road bridges of a great span. If wanted for a common road, and the span be not more than 150 feet, the arch beam may be safely dispensed with; and in that case, counter braces should be introduced; but if the bridge be designed for a railroad, the arch beam should never be omitted.

The panels of bridges of this kind ought never to be as great in extension as in height between chords; or, in other words, the rise of the braces should always be greater than their run; and practically, it is expensive and inconvenient to extend the panels more than 12 or 14 feet. In all bridges of this kind, the greatest strain upon the braces is at the end of the span; and it will be most proper to use the best and largest pieces of timber for the end braces, and those of inferior quality, if such must be used somewhere, should be placed in the middle.

The posts should be sized down at the lower end, where they pass through the lower chord, to about 6 inches in thickness; the chord pieces should also be cut out to the depth of 1 inch on each side of the post, and both locked into the post in the firmest possible manner, in order to resist the thrust of the brace. The post should also be boxed into the upper chord not less than 1 inch.

In scarfing the lower chord pieces, they must be so arranged that only one splice be made at the same place; and if the bolts which pass through the scarfing extend also through both lower chord pieces, (the short piece inserted to lock the joint being of just sufficient thickness to fill the space between the two chord pieces), it would be still better than that plan represented in the Plate.

It will be found necessary, in a bridge of this kind, to make the main braces at least $1\frac{1}{4}$ inches longer than the exact calculation would require, in order to produce the necessary camber, and to guard against the settling of the centre of the span below the general level, which will be likely to happen if not guarded against, from the com-

Plate 36.

Arch Beam & Posts.

Brace

150 feet

Cross Section

Post.

Lower Chord.

Scarfing in Lower Chord.

pression and shrinkage of the timber, and which would materially weaken the bridge; and whatever camber the bridge is designed to have, must be given to it on its first erection, before the false works are removed, since the camber cannot afterward be increased as it can be in most of the bridges represented on the preceding Plates, where supporting rods, in those plans, occupy the place of the posts in this.

For floor plan, see Plate 37.

Bill of Timber for One Span.

2 Wall plates,	10 by 12 in.,	22 feet long,	B. M.=	440 feet.
8 Lower chord pieces,	7 by 14 "	34 "	"	"	=	2286 "
8 " " "	7 by 14 "	43 "	"	"	=	2809 "
4 Upper " "	11 by 11 "	36 "	"	"	=	1452 "
4 " " "	11 by 11 "	44 "	"	"	=	1774 "
46 Floor beams,	4 by 12 "	20 "	"	"	=	3680 "
60 Arch pieces,	7 by 10 "	33 "	"	"	=11550 "
12 Queen posts,	11 by 15 "	19 "	"	"	=	3135 "
8 " "	11 by 14 "	19 "	"	"	=	1950 "
8 " "	11 by 13 "	19 "	"	"	=	1811 "
2 Centre posts,	11 by 16 "	19 "	"	"	=	557 "
4 Arch braces,	12 by 14 "	18 "	"	"	=	1008 "
28 Panel girths,	6 by 8 "	11 "	"	"	=	1232 "
12 Scarfing blocks,	6 by 14 "	5 "	"	"	=	420 "
16 Tie beams,	10 by 10 "	19 "	"	"	=	2533 "
32 Knee braces,	4 by 6 "	6 "	"	"	=	384 "
18 Lateral braces,	4 by 8 "	24 "	"	"	=	1152 "
7000 feet 3 inch floor plank,		14 "	"	"	=	7000 "

Bill of Iron.

9 Cross rods,	1 in. diam.	19 feet 3 inches long	=460 lbs.
22 Arch bolts,	1 "	2 " 9 "	"	=160 "
24 Splice bolts,	1 "	1 foot 8 "	"	=106 "
30 Post bolts,	1 "	1 " 8 "	"	=132 "
60 Arch bolts,	¾ "	2 feet 0 "	"	=179 "
Head, nut, and washer to each bolt, 1 lb. each,				345 "

PLATE 37.

This Plate represents an ordinary Howe Bridge, with the addition of two arch beams to each truss. The arch beams are combined with the truss by supporting rods, extending downward between each panel from the upper surface of the arch and through the angle block to the lower surface of the lower chords. As another modification of the Howe Bridge has been already described in Plate 32, and as the arrangement of the arch beams in this design is similar to that represented in Plate 36, it will only be necessary, in this place, to add a bill of timber and iron, which, with the inspection of the various figures of the Plate, will be sufficient to enable any practical carpenter to understand the construction of this bridge.

Bill of Timber for One Span.

2 Wall plates,	10 by 12 in.,	20 feet long, B. M.	=	400 feet.
4 Bolsters,	10 by 12 "	22 " " "	=	880 "
8 Pier braces,	7 by 7 "	18 " " "	=	588 "
16 Lower chords,	5 by 12 "	45 " " "	=	3600 "
16 " "	5 by 12 "	41 " " "	=	3280 "
12 Upper "	6 by 10 "	45 " " "	=	2700 "
12 " "	6 by 10 "	41 " " "	=	2460 "
64 Main braces,	6 by 8 "	19 " " "	=	4864 "
32 Counter "	6 by 7 "	19 " " "	=	2128 "
80 Arch pieces,	7 by 10 "	36 " " "	=	16800 "
34 Cross floor timbers,	7 by 14 "	19 " " "	=	5276 "
32 Lateral braces,	4 by 8 "	24 " " "	=	2048 "
8 Rail stringers,	7 by 14 "	45 " " "	=	2940 "
"	7 by 14 "	41 " " "	=	2679 "

Bill of Iron for One Span.

Castings.

30 Lower chord angle blocks,	80 lbs. each,	=2400 lbs
30 Upper " " "	75 "	=2250 "
8 Half angle blocks,	50 "	= 400 "
44 Arch rod washers,	3 "	= 132 "
282 Washers,	1 "	= 282 "

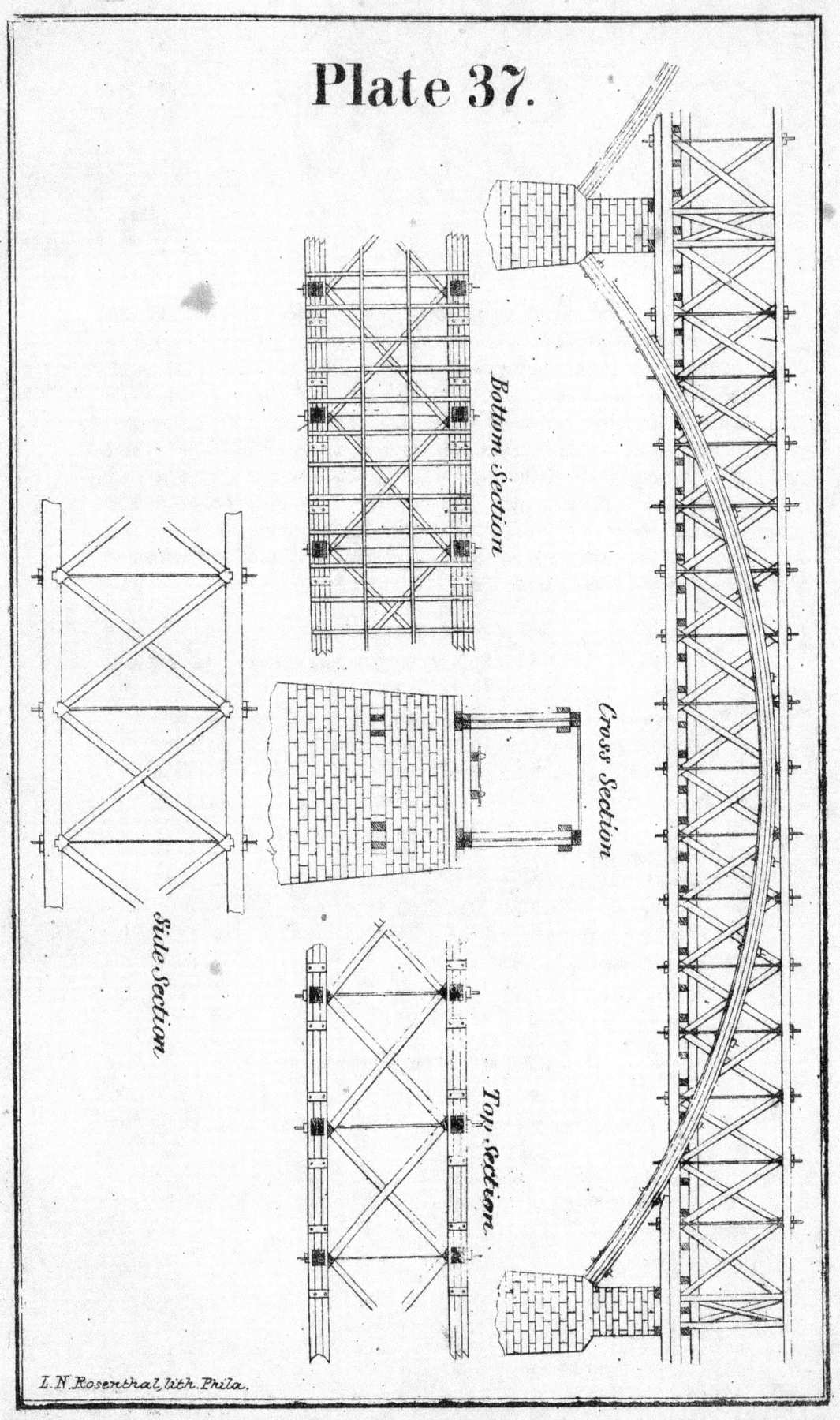

Wrought Iron.

8 End supporting rods,	$1\frac{1}{2}$ in. diam.,	$19\frac{1}{2}$ feet long,	= 930 lbs.
16 " " "	$1\frac{1}{2}$ "	$18\frac{1}{2}$ " "	=1775 "
24 " " "	$1\frac{1}{4}$ "	$18\frac{1}{2}$ " "	=1865 "
12 Middle "	$1\frac{1}{8}$ "	$18\frac{1}{2}$ " "	= 755 "
8 Arch " "	$1\frac{1}{4}$ "	$6\frac{1}{2}$ " "	= 218 "
8 " " "	$1\frac{1}{4}$ "	$10\frac{2}{3}$ " "	= 361 "
8 " " "	$1\frac{3}{8}$ "	$13\frac{1}{2}$ " "	= 540 "
8 " " "	$1\frac{3}{8}$ "	15 " "	= 600 "
8 " " "	$1\frac{3}{8}$ "	16 " "	= 640 "
4 " " "	$1\frac{3}{8}$ "	17 " "	= 320 "
9 Top cross rods,	1 "	19 " "	= 460 "
9 Bottom cross rods,	1 "	$19\frac{1}{3}$ " "	= 470 "
64 Upper chord bolts,	$\frac{3}{4}$ "	21 in "	= 168 "
64 Lower " "	$\frac{3}{4}$ "	23 " "	= 183 "
52 Arch beam bolts,	$\frac{3}{4}$ "	30 " "	= 195 "
28 " cross bolts,	$\frac{3}{4}$ "	40 " "	= 140 "
32 Main brace bolts,	$\frac{3}{4}$ "	20 " "	= 80 "
32 Rail stringer bolts,	$\frac{3}{4}$ "	16 " "	= 64 "
208 Large nuts and heads,	3 lbs. each		= 624 "
540 Small " "	1 lb. "		= 540 "
22 Bottom gibs, 4 holes,	40 lbs. "		= 880 "
8 " " 2 holes,	31 " "		= 320 "
30 Top " 2 "	5 " "		= 750 "

Estimate of Cost.

The entire cost of a bridge of this kind in the State of Illinois is about $25 per lineal foot

PLATE 38.

This bridge is similar, in its general principles of construction, to the one represented in Plate 37; but is quite different in its minor details, being much heavier and stronger, as well as more expensive. The main differences are these: Counter braces are employed in this bridge, which are omitted in the other; this has two sets of posts and main braces, and but one arch beam to each truss, while the other bridge has two arch beams and one set of posts and braces; the chord pieces in this bridge, instead of being placed side by side, with their edges vertical, with an open space between them for the circulation of air, are placed one upon the other, with their edges horizontal, and their surfaces in close contact.

The upper chord is in three sections, and the lower chord and the arch beam are each in four sections; each chord piece and arch piece being 6 inches deep and 12 inches wide; making the combined upper chord 12 by 18 inches, and the combined lower chord and arch beam each 12 by 24 inches.

The foot of the arch beam rests upon a cast iron shoe, secured by iron straps to each of the lower chord pieces; each shoe having four flanges, and each flange beveled to fit the square end of each section of the arch beam.

There is one set of counter braces to each truss, each counter brace passing between each pair of main braces, to which it is bolted at their intersection. The foot of each counter brace rests upon an angle block fixed upon the lower chord, at the foot of each pair of posts, and the upper end of each counter brace rests against the arch beam at its intersection with the next pair of posts. A key is inserted, however, between the upper end of each counter brace and the arch beam, by means of which the whole structure can be kept tight, and the relative strain upon the arch beam and the chords can, to some extent, be regulated and proportioned. Each pair of posts is bolted together with four bolts—one above, and one below each chord.

Bridges of this style are in extensive use on the New York and Erie Rail-road, where they have been proved to be of great strength and stability.

Plate 38.

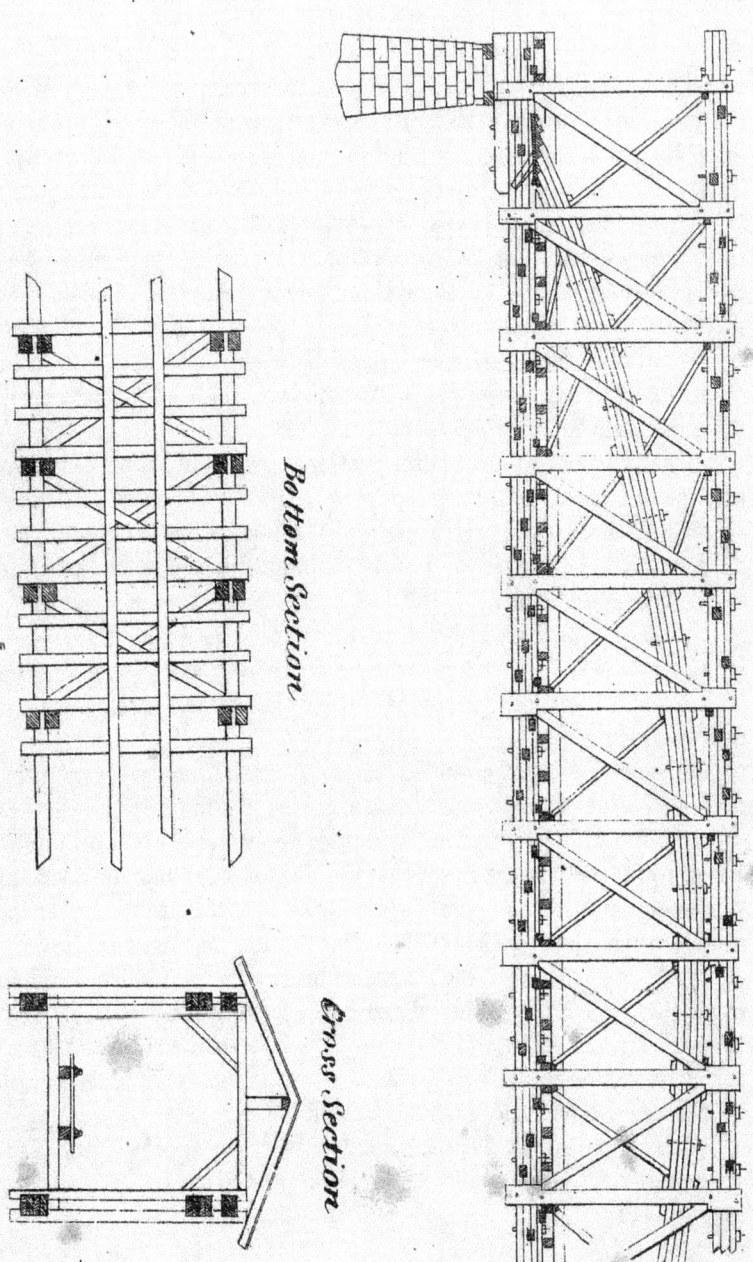

Bottom Section

Cross Section

GENERAL PRINCIPLES OF BRIDGE BUILDING.

In concluding this Part of the work, it is proper to bring together into one place the most important principles and most useful hints to practical builders, which we have been able to gather, either from the study of other works,* or from the lessons of our own experience.

Size of Timber and Iron required to enable a Bridge of a given Span to sustain a given Load.

The most proper way of ascertaining the resisting powers of timber and iron is by actual experiment; and it has been found by such experiment, that the greatest safe strain for sound timber is about 1,000 lbs. per square inch, measured on the square end of the timber, the strain being one of either extension or compression, but applied in the direction of the grain of the wood. It has also been ascertained by experiment, that the greatest safe *tensile strain*, as it is technically called, that is the lifting or supporting strain, of large wrought iron rods, is 10,000 lbs. per square inch. Small wire or nail rods, manufactured with more care, and of the best materials, can, undoubtedly, sustain a much greater weight than this.

In proportioning the different parts of a bridge, however, it is customary and expedient to allow a considerable excess of strength in favor of stability. The deterioration of timber, caused by age, must be taken into the account; for after a wooden bridge has been in use for some years, it becomes much weaker than when first erected.

The weight of the bridge itself must also be considered in determining the load which it is able to sustain, and this weight it is considered safe to assume at 35 lbs. to the cubic foot of timber employed. If the quantity of timber in a given bridge is equal to 30 cubic feet to every foot in length, as is asserted by Haupt to be the case with the average of the Howe Bridges on the Pennsylvania Rail-road, then the weight of the structure would be 1050 lbs. per lineal foot, or a

---

* Many of these remarks are condensed and simplified from the work on "Bridge Construction," by Herman Haupt, A. M.—D. Appleton & Co., New York, a work more especially designed for the use of engineers than for practical builders, yet one which we commend to all persons interested in this part of Carpentry.

little more than half a ton per foot for the weight of the timber, exclusive of the iron.

The greatest load that can be brought upon a rail-road bridge, with a single track, is when several locomotive engines of the first class, weighing about one ton per foot in length, are attached together. So that the greatest strain upon such a bridge, including both its own weight and the weight of the load, is a little more than a ton and a half per foot. What, then, must be the dimensions of the timber to resist this strain?

The Strain upon the Chords.

When a beam is supported at the ends and loaded in the middle until it breaks, it is observed that the fibres in the lower portion of the fracture are broken by being extended or pulled violently apart, and that those on the upper portion are broken by being compressed or jammed violently together. In theory, this compression is said to be equal to the expansion; that is, that it will require an equal force to tear the fibres apart as to break them by forcing them together, and the neutral axis in the beam, or the line where there is neither sufficient expansion nor compression to break the fibres of the timber, is said to be in the middle of the beam. But it is doubtful whether facts will warrant this conclusion. Common observation would lead most persons to the opinion that timber has a greater power to resist compression than it has to resist expansion, and to this opinion we are ourselves inclined; but for the present purposes it will be sufficiently accurate to be governed by the theory usually adopted by engineers, as stated.

The power of a bridge to sustain a load, and to resist the various strains upon it, may be compared to that of the beam supported at the ends—the strain on the upper chord being one of compression, and that on the lower chord one of extension; and the strain on both being greatest in the middle of the span, and diminishing toward the ends. When the beam is laid over several supports, its strength for a given interval is much greater than when simply supported at the ends. The same principle is applicable to bridges; and when several spans occur in succession, it is of great advantage to continue the upper and lower chords across the piers.

The greatest strain on the upper chord being in the middle of the span, is equal to that force which, being applied horizontally, would sustain one half the span with its load were the other half to be re moved. In order to ascertain this force, multiply half the span and its load by one fourth its length, and divide that product by its height, measured from centre to centre of the upper and lower chords.

For example, if the length of a span be 160 feet, and the height of the truss be 16 feet from centre to centre of upper and lower chords, and the weight of the loaded bridge be 1½ tons to the lineal foot, the greatest strain upon the upper chord would be expressed by the product of 120 tons multiplied by 40, and the product divided by 16; which gives 300 tons, or 600,000 lbs. as the result. The reason of multiplying the weight of half the loaded span by 40 is, because 40 feet is the middle of the half-span, or its centre of gravity; and the reason for dividing its product by 16 is, because that is the width of the truss; and the wider the truss, the greater leverage there is, and the less strain, for the same reason that a thick beam is stronger than a flat one, as there is less strain on the upper and lower surfaces of the thick beam from the same weight than in a flat one. Then, as each square inch is able to resist 1000 lbs., there must be 600 square inches in the end section of the upper chords, in order to enable them to sustain the weight required, or 300 inches in the upper chord of each truss. If, therefore, each chord is 12 inches deep, it must be 25 inches wide; hence, three chord pieces, 12 by 8⅓ inches, will contain the requisite material

The strain on the lower chord is at least equal to that on the upper one; but the timbers being in several pieces, and the strain being one of extension, the joints are opened, and the whole strength of the timber is not available; while in the upper chord the strain is one of compression, and the joints being pressed together, causes no loss to the resisting force of the timber. There must, therefore, be at least one additional line of timbers in the lower chord; and each piece should be sufficiently long to extend through four panels, so that there can be three whole timbers and a joint in each panel.

From the same data, similar calculations can easily be made for estimating the strain and fixing the dimensions of the other timbers.

PART IV.

EXPLANATION OF THE TABLES.

Definitions of Terms and Phrases used in this Explanation, and in other Places in this Work.

The LENGTH *of a rafter* is understood to be measured from the extreme point of the foot to the extreme point of its upper end.* But in these Tables no allowances are made for the projection of rafters beyond the plate, or for ridge poles; so that the *length of common rafters is understood to be the distance from the upper and outer corner of the plate to the very peak of the roof.*

The RUN *of a rafter* is the horizontal distance from the extreme point of the foot to a perpendicular let fall from the upper end. *In common roofs, the run of the rafters is half the width of the building.*

The RISE *of a rafter* is the perpendicular distance from the upper end of the rafter to the level of the foot.

The GAIN *of a rafter* is the difference between its *run* and its *length*. For example, a rafter whose run is 12 feet, and whose length is 13 feet, has 1 foot gain.

The learner will easily perceive that the length of any rafter is the hypotenuse of a right-angled triangle, of which its run and its rise are the other two sides. The length is therefore ascertained with perfect accuracy by adding the square of the run to the square of the rise, and extracting the square root of their sum. (See Part I., Prop. XXIV.)

Example 1. The length of a common rafter is required in a building 24 feet wide, the roof of which is desired to have a pitch of 5 inches to the foot. The *run* is therefore 12 feet, the square of which

---

* Except in *hip rafters*, the length of which is always to be measured on the *backing*, or along the middle line of the upper surface; for when the side bevel is all cut on one side of the upper end, as it sometimes is, then the point of the rafter will extend half its thickness beyond its estimated length, as given in the table, &c.

114   CARPENTRY MADE EASY.

is the product of 12 multiplied by 12, or 144 feet. The *rise* is 12 times 5 inches, or 60 inches, or 5 feet, the square of which is 25 feet; which, added to 144, makes 169 feet, of which we extract the square root *thus*:

(the rule for which may be found in any common-school arithmetic) and find it to be 13 feet, the exact length of the rafter required.

```
1)169(13
  1
  ──
 23)69
    69
    ──
    00
```

But in most cases the result is obtained in the form of a fraction; and it will be found convenient to reduce the *run* and the *rise* to inches, in the first place, and then the root is obtained in inches and decimals of an inch, which can be carried out to any degree of accuracy required. In these Tables they are carried to hundredths of an inch.

Example 2. Required the length of a rafter for the building described in Plate 4 of this work. Width of building, 12 feet; rise of rafter, 6 inches to the foot.

The *run* of the rafter is 6 feet, or 72 in., of which the square is   5184
" *rise* " " " 3 " or 36 " " " " "   1296

and their *sum* is   6480

of which we proceed to extract the square root *thus*: and find it to be 80 inches and 49 hundredths of an inch; or, 6 feet 8 inches and $\frac{49}{100}$, as given in the Table, which is the exact length of the required rafter.

```
8)6480(80.49
  64
  ──
 1604)8000
      6416
      ────
    16089)158400
          144801
          ──────
           13599
```

TABLE I.

The use of this Table is to furnish the practical carpenter with the precise lengths of common rafters for buildings of all sizes, and for roofs of every pitch. The Table is carried out to buildings of 60 feet in width; but should the length of rafters for a wider building be required, it will be necessary to add such numbers together in the left-hand column as will make their sum equal to the width of the building, and then the sum of the lengths of the rafters given in the Table opposite these numbers, thus added together, will be the true length of the rafters required.

For example, suppose it were required to find the length of rafters for a building 84 feet wide, 6 inches rise. We find the length of a rafter of half that width, of the same pitch, to be 23 ft. 5.74 in., and double this number would be the length of the rafter required, or 46 ft. 11.48 in.

Example 2. Required the length of the rafters for a building 102 feet wide, 5 inches rise. We perceive that 50 and 52 added together will make 102. The lengths of these two dimensions for this pitch, as given in the Table, are 27 ft. 1 in., and 28 ft. 2 in., the sum of which is 55 ft. 3 in., the length of the rafters required.

CARPENTRY MADE EASY.

TABLE I.

Length of Rafters in Feet, Inches, and Hundredths of an Inch. Rise of Rafter to the Foot in Inches.

Width of Building in Feet.	Run of Rafter.	1 inch Rise.	2 inch Rise.	3 inch Rise.	4 inch Rise.	5 inch Rise.	6 inch Rise.	7 inch Rise.	8 inch Rise.	9 inch Rise.
4	2	2 : 0.08	2 : 0.33	2 : 0.73	2 : 1.29	2 : 2.00	2 : 2.83	2 : 3.78	2 : 4.84	2 : 6
5	2 : 6	2 : 6.10	2 : 6.41	2 : 6.92	2 : 7.62	2 : 8.50	2 : 9.54	2 : 10.73	3 : 0.05	3 : 1.50
6	3	3 : 0.12	3 : 0.49	3 : 1.10	3 : 1.94	3 : 3	3 : 4.24	3 : 5.67	3 : 7.26	3 : 9
7	3 : 6	3 : 6.14	3 : 6.57	3 : 7.30	3 : 8.27	3 : 9.50	3 : 10.95	4 : 0.62	4 : 2.47	4 : 4.50
8	4	4 : 0.16	4 : 0.66	4 : 1.47	4 : 2.59	4 : 4	4 : 5.66	4 : 7.56	4 : 9.68	5 :
9	4 : 6	4 : 6.18	4 : 6.74	4 : 7.66	4 : 8.92	4 : 10.50	5 : 0.36	5 : 2.51	5 : 4.89	5 : 7.50
10	5	5 : 0.20	5 : 0.82	5 : 1.84	5 : 3.24	5 : 5	5 : 7.08	5 : 9.45	6 : 0.10	6 : 3
11	5 : 6	5 : 6.22	5 : 6.91	5 : 8.03	5 : 9.57	5 : 11.50	6 : 1.78	6 : 4.41	6 : 7.31	6 : 10.50
12	6	6 : 0.25	6 : 0.99	6 : 2.21	6 : 3.89	6 : 6	6 : 8.49	6 : 11.34	7 : 2.52	7 : 6
14	7	7 : 0.29	7 : 1.15	7 : 2.58	7 : 4.54	7 : 7	7 : 9.91	8 : 1.23	8 : 5.94	8 : 9
16	8	8 : 0.33	8 : 1.32	8 : 2.95	8 : 5.19	8 : 8	8 : 11.32	9 : 3.12	9 : 7.36	10 :
18	9	9 : 0.36	9 : 1.48	9 : 3.32	9 : 5.84	9 : 9	10 : 0.74	10 : 5.03	10 : 9.79	11 : 3
20	10	10 : 0.40	10 : 1.64	10 : 3.69	10 : 6.49	10 : 10	11 : 2.16	11 : 6.92	12 : 0.22	12 : 6
22	11	11 : 0.44	11 : 1.81	11 : 4.06	11 : 7.14	11 : 11	12 : 3.58	12 : 8.81	13 : 2.64	13 : 9
24	12	12 : 0.49	12 : 1.98	12 : 4.43	12 : 7.79	13 :	13 : 4.99	13 : 10.70	14 : 5.06	15 :
26	13	13 : 0.53	13 : 2.15	13 : 4.80	13 : 8.44	14 : 1	14 : 6.41	15 : 0.59	15 : 7.48	16 : 3
28	14	14 : 0.57	14 : 2.31	14 : 5.17	14 : 9.09	15 : 2	15 : 7.82	16 : 2.48	16 : 9.90	17 : 6
30	15	15 : 0.62	15 : 2.48	15 : 5.54	15 : 9.73	16 : 3	16 : 9.24	17 : 4.38	18 : 0.32	18 : 9
32	16	16 : 0.66	16 : 2.64	16 : 5.91	16 : 10.38	17 : 4	17 : 10.65	18 : 6.27	19 : 2.74	20 :
34	17	17 : 0.70	17 : 2.80	17 : 6.28	17 : 11.03	18 : 5	19 : 0.07	19 : 8.16	20 : 5.16	21 : 3
36	18	18 : 0.73	18 : 2.96	18 : 6.65	18 : 11.68	19 : 6	20 : 1.48	20 : 10.06	21 : 7.58	22 : 6
38	19	19 : 0.78	19 : 3.12	19 : 7.02	20 : 0.33	20 : 7	21 : 2.90	21 : 11.95	22 : 10	23 : 9
40	20	20 : 0.81	20 : 3.28	20 : 7.39	21 : 0.98	21 : 8	22 : 4.32	23 : 1.85	24 : 0.43	25 :
42	21	21 : 0.85	21 : 3.45	21 : 7.76	22 : 1.63	22 : 9	23 : 5.74	24 : 3.74	25 : 2.85	26 : 3
44	22	22 : 0.89	22 : 3.62	22 : 8.12	23 : 2.28	23 : 10	24 : 7.16	25 : 5.64	26 : 5.27	27 : 6
46	23	23 : 0.93	23 : 3.79	23 : 8.49	24 : 2.93	24 : 11	25 : 8.58	26 : 7.53	27 : 7.69	28 : 9
48	24	24 : 0.97	24 : 3.96	24 : 8.86	25 : 3.57	26 :	26 : 10	27 : 9.42	28 : 10.12	30 :
50	25	25 : 1.01	25 : 4.13	25 : 9.23	26 : 4.22	27 : 1	27 : 11.41	28 : 11.31	30 : 0.54	31 : 3
52	26	26 : 1.06	26 : 4.30	26 : 9.60	27 : 4.87	28 : 2	29 : 0.83	30 : 1.20	31 : 2.96	32 : 6
54	27	27 : 1.10	27 : 4.46	27 : 9.97	28 : 5.52	29 : 3	30 : 2.24	31 : 3.09	32 : 5.39	33 : 9
56	28	28 : 1.14	28 : 4.63	28 : 10.34	29 : 6.17	30 : 4	31 : 3.66	32 : 4.98	33 : 7.81	35 :
58	29	29 : 1.18	29 : 4.79	29 : 10.71	30 : 6.82	31 : 5	32 : 5.08	33 : 6.87	34 : 10.24	36 : 3
60	30	30 : 1.23	30 : 4.96	30 : 11.08	31 : 7.47	32 : 6	33 : 6.49	34 : 8.76	36 : 0.66	37 : 6

EXPLANATION OF TABLES.

TABLE I.—*Continued.*

Length of Rafters in Feet, Inches, and Hundredths of an Inch. Rise of Rafter to the Foot in Inches.

Width of Building in Feet.	Run of Rafter.	10 inch Rise.	11 inch Rise.	12 inch Rise.	13 inch Rise.	14 inch Rise.	15 inch Rise.	16 inch Rise.	17 inch Rise.	18 inch Rise.
4	2	2: 7.24	2: 8.55	2: 9.94	2: 11.38	2: 0.87	3: 2.41	3: 4	3: 5.61	3: 7.26
5	2:6	3: 3.05	3: 4.69	3: 6.42	3: 8.22	3: 10.09	4: 0.02	4: 2	4: 4.02	4: 6.08
6	3	3: 10.86	4: 0.83	4: 2.91	4: 5.07	4: 7.31	4: 9.62	5:	5: 2.42	5: 4.89
7	3:6	4: 6.67	4: 8.97	4: 11.39	5: 1.92	5: 4.53	5: 7.23	5:10	6: 0.82	6: 3.71
8	4	5: 2.48	5: 5.11	5: 7.88	5: 10.76	6: 1.75	6: 4.83	6: 8	6: 11.23	7: 2.53
9	4:6	5: 10.29	6: 1.25	6: 4.36	6: 7.61	6: 10.97	7: 2.44	7: 6	7: 9.63	8: 1.34
10	5	6: 6.10	6: 9.39	7: 0.85	7: 4.45	7: 8.19	8: 0.04	8: 4	8: 8.04	9: 0.16
11	5:6	7: 1.91	7: 5.53	7: 9.33	8: 1.30	8: 5.41	8: 9.65	9: 2	9: 6.44	9: 10.98
12	6	7: 9.72	8: 1.67	8: 5.82	8: 10.15	9: 2.63	9: 7.25	10:	10: 4.84	10: 9.79
14	7	9: 1.34	9: 5.95	9: 10.79	10: 3.84	10: 9.07	11: 2.46	11: 8	12: 1.65	12: 7.43
16	8	10: 4.96	10: 10.23	11: 3.76	11: 9.53	12: 3.51	12: 9.67	13: 4	13: 10.46	14: 5.06
18	9	11: 8.58	12: 2.51	12: 8.73	13: 3.22	13: 9.95	14: 4.88	15:	15: 7.27	16: 2.69
20	10	13: 0.20	13: 6.79	14: 1.70	14: 8.91	15: 4.39	16: 0.09	16: 8	17: 4.08	18: 0.33
22	11	14: 3.82	14: 11.07	15: 6.67	16: 2.60	16: 10.83	17: 7.30	18: 4	19: 0.88	19: 9.96
24	12	15: 7.44	16: 3.34	16: 11.64	17: 8.30	18: 5.27	19: 2.51	20:	20: 9.69	21: 7.59
26	13	16: 11.06	17: 7.62	18: 4.61	19: 1.99	19: 11.71	20: 9.72	21: 8	22: 6.50	23: 5.22
28	14	18: 2.68	18: 11.90	19: 9.58	20: 7.67	21: 6.14	22: 4.93	23: 4	24: 3.31	25: 2.86
30	15	19: 6.30	20: 4.18	21: 2.55	22: 1.37	23: 0.58	24: 0.14	25:	26: 0.12	27: 0.49
32	16	20: 9.92	21: 8.46	22: 7.52	23: 7.07	24: 7.02	25: 7.35	26: 8	27: 8.92	28: 10.12
34	17	22: 1.54	23: 0.74	24: 0.49	25: 0.77	26: 1.46	27: 2.56	28: 4	29: 5.73	30: 7.76
36	18	23: 5.16	24: 5.02	25: 5.47	26: 6.46	27: 7.90	28: 9.77	30:	31: 2.55	32: 5.39
38	19	24: 8.78	25: 9.30	26: 10.44	28: 0.15	29: 2.34	30: 4.98	31: 8	32: 11.36	34: 3.02
40	20	26: 0.40	27: 1.57	28: 3.41	29: 5.84	30: 8.70	32: 0.19	33: 4	34: 8.17	36: 0.66
42	21	27: 4.02	28: 5.85	29: 8.38	30: 11.53	32: 3.22	33: 7.39	35:	36: 4.97	37: 10.29
44	22	28: 7.64	29: 10.13	31: 1.35	32: 5.22	33: 9.66	35: 2.60	36: 8	38: 1.78	39: 7.92
46	23	29: 11.26	31: 2.41	32: 6.32	33: 10.92	35: 4.10	36: 9.81	38: 4	39: 10.59	41: 5.55
48	24	31: 2.88	32: 6.69	33: 11.29	35: 4.61	36: 10.54	38: 5.02	40:	41: 7.40	43: 3.19
50	25	32: 6.50	33: 10.97	35: 4.26	36: 10.30	38: 4.98	40: 0.23	41: 8	43: 4.21	45: 0.82
52	26	33: 10.12	35: 3.25	36: 9.23	38: 3.99	39: 11.42	41: 7.44	43: 4	45: 1.01	46: 10.45
54	27	35: 1.74	36: 7.53	38: 2.20	39: 9.08	41: 5.86	43: 2.65	45:	46: 9.82	48: 8.09
56	28	36: 5.36	37: 11.80	39: 7.17	41: 3.37	43: 0.30	44: 9.86	46: 8	48: 6.63	50: 5.72
58	29	37: 8.98	39: 4.08	41: 0.14	42: 9.06	44: 6.74	46: 5.07	48: 4	50: 3.44	52: 3.35
60	30	39: 0.60	40: 8.36	42: 5.11	44: 2.75	46: 1.18	48: 0.28	50:	52: 0.25	54: 0.99

TABLE II.

Length of Hip Rafters.

If a roof were perfectly horizontal or flat, the hip rafters would each be equal to the diagonal of a square, having for its side half the width of the building; and the square root of twice the square of half the side, would, in that case, be the length of the hip rafter. This we call the RUN *of the hip rafter*. But if the roof has any pitch, the *length* of the rafter is greater than its *run*, and is always equal to the hypotenuse of a right-angled triangle, having the *run* for a base, and the *rise* for a perpendicular; and the length is found, as in common rafters, by adding the square of the run to the square of the rise, and extracting the square root of the sum.

Two calculations are necessary according to the above demonstration: First, for obtaining the *run;* and secondly, having found the run, from that to obtain the *length*.

First. Suppose the width of the building to be 40 feet, and the rise of the roof 5 inches to the foot, or 100 inches; then half the width of the building, 20 feet, is 240 inches, the square of which is 57,600. Double this number (for the two sides of the square) is 115,200 inches, of which the square root is $339\frac{41}{100}$ inches, or, 28 ft. $3\frac{41}{100}$ in., which is the *run of the hip rafter*.

Second. To obtain the *length*, which equals the hypotenuse of a right-angled triangle, of which the run is the base and the rise the perpendicular.

The *run* is 339.41 inches as obtained above,

The square of which is	115,200
The rise is 100 inches, of which the square is	10,000

The sum of these two squares is 125,200 inches, of which the square root is 353.83 inches, or 29 ft. 5.83 in., which is the true *length of the hip rafter*.

The process of obtaining the length is explained above according to the *long way*, and the most obvious and analytical way also, and one which every practical mechanic should make himself fully familiar with: but *practically*, the process may be shortened as follows:—

EXPLANATION OF TABLES.

Add the square of the rise to twice the square of half the width, and the square root of the sum will be length of hip rafter required. Thus:—

The square of the rise (100 inches) is	10,000
Twice the square of half the width is	115,200
Their sum is	125,200

of which the square root is 353.83 in., or 29 ft. 5.83 in. as before; which is the true length of the hip rafter as measured on the backing. See note on p. 113.

TABLE II.
Length of Hip Rafters in Feet, Inches, and Hundredths of an Inch.

Width of Building in feet.	Run of Rafter.	1 inch Rise.	2 inch Rise.	3 inch Rise.	4 inch Rise.	5 inch Rise.	6 inch Rise.	7 inch Rise.	8 inch Rise.
4	2 : 9.94	2 : 10	2 : 10.17	2 : 10.46	2 : 10.87	2 : 11.38	3 :	3 : 0.71	3 : 1.52
5	3 : 6.42	3 : 6.50	3 : 6.72	3 : 7.08	3 : 7.58	3 : 8.22	3 : 9	3 : 9.89	3 : 10.90
6	4 : 2.91	4 : 3	4 : 3.26	4 : 3.70	4 : 4.30	4 : 5.07	4 : 6	4 : 7.07	4 : 8.28
7	4 : 11.39	4 : 11.50	4 : 11.80	5 : 0.31	5 : 1.02	5 : 1.92	5 : 3	5 : 4.25	5 : 5.66
8	5 : 7.88	5 : 8	5 : 8.35	5 : 8.93	5 : 9.74	5 : 10.76	6 :	6 : 1.43	6 : 3.04
9	6 : 4.36	6 : 4.50	6 : 4.89	6 : 5.55	6 : 6.46	6 : 7.61	6 : 9	6 : 10.60	7 : 0.42
10	7 : 0.85	7 : 1	7 : 1.44	7 : 2.16	7 : 3.17	7 : 4.45	7 : 6	7 : 7.78	7 : 9.80
11	7 : 9.33	7 : 9.50	7 : 9.98	7 : 10.78	7 : 11.89	8 : 1.30	8 : 3	8 : 4.96	8 : 7.18
12	8 : 5.82	8 : 6	8 : 6.52	8 : 7.39	8 : 8.61	8 : 10.15	9 :	9 : 2.14	9 : 4.56
14	9 : 10.79	9 : 11	9 : 11.61	10 : 0.63	10 : 2.04	10 : 3.84	10 : 6	10 : 8.50	10 : 11.33
16	11 : 3.76	11 : 4	11 : 4.70	11 : 5.86	11 : 7.48	11 : 9.53	12 :	12 : 2.86	12 : 6.09
18	12 : 8.73	12 : 9	12 : 9.79	12 : 11.09	13 : 0.91	13 : 3.22	13 : 6	13 : 9.21	14 : 0.85
20	14 : 1.70	14 : 2	14 : 2.88	14 : 4.33	14 : 6.35	14 : 8.91	15 :	15 : 3.57	15 : 7.61
22	15 : 6.67	15 : 7	15 : 7.96	15 : 9.57	15 : 11.79	16 : 2.60	16 : 6	16 : 9.93	17 : 2.37
24	16 : 11.64	17 :	17 : 1.05	17 : 2.80	17 : 5.22	17 : 8.30	18 :	18 : 4.29	18 : 9.34
26	18 : 4.61	18 : 5	18 : 6.14	18 : 8.03	18 : 10.66	19 : 1.99	19 : 6	19 : 10.64	20 : 3.90
28	19 : 9.58	19 : 10	19 : 11.23	20 : 1.26	20 : 4.09	20 : 7.68	21 :	21 : 5	21 : 10.66
30	21 : 2.55	21 : 3	21 : 4.32	21 : 6.50	21 : 9.53	22 : 1.37	22 : 6	22 : 11.36	23 : 5.42
32	22 : 7.52	22 : 8	22 : 9.40	22 : 11.73	23 : 2.96	23 : 7.06	24 :	24 : 5.72	24 : 11.18
34	24 : 0.49	24 : 1	24 : 2.49	24 : 4.97	24 : 8.40	25 : 0.76	25 : 6	26 : 0.07	26 : 5.94
36	25 : 5.46	25 : 6	25 : 7.58	25 : 10.20	26 : 1.83	26 : 6.45	27 :	27 : 6.43	28 : 0.70
38	26 : 10.44	26 : 11	27 : 0.67	27 : 3.43	27 : 7.27	28 : 0.14	28 : 6	29 : 0.79	29 : 7.47
40	28 : 3.41	28 : 4	28 : 5.76	28 : 8.27	29 : 0.71	29 : 5.83	30 :	30 : 7.15	31 : 2.23

TABLE III.

Hip and Jack Rafters on Octagonal Roofs.

The length of one side of an octagonal building being commonly given as the basis of calculation in framing, it will first be necessary from this basis, to determine with accuracy the width of the building from the middle of one side to the middle of the opposite side; and also the diagonal width, from one corner to the opposite corner.

The width FG (in Plate 20, Fig. 1) is obviously the same as one side of the circumscribed square DE; and DE is made up of three parts, namely, DA, AB, and BE, one of which parts, AB, is known—being a side of the given octagon. The other two parts are equal to each other, namely, DA=BE.* We have, therefore, to find the length of DA, to double it, and to add AB to it in order to ascertain the width of the building. The length of DA is found as follows:—

In the right-angled triangle CAD, the hypotenuse AC, being one of the sides of the given octagon, is known; and the square of this hypotenuse is equal to the sum of the squares of the other two sides DA and DC, or to double the square of DA.

For example, suppose the sides of the regular octagon be given equal to 16 feet, which, on reducing it to inches to insure greater accuracy, is 192 inches.

The square of 192 inches is 36,864 inches, one half which is 18,432 inches, which is the square of DA.

The square root of 18,432 inches is 135.76 inches, or 11 ft. 3.76 in., the length of DA.

Double this number (for DA×BE), and add 16 feet for the length of AB, and we have 38 ft. 7.52 in., *the width of the building.*

The *diagonal width* is obtained as follows:

Let O' represent the point at the foot of the perpendicular let fall

---

* The equality of DA and BE may be demonstrated thus:—Suppose the figure divided into two parts by the line FG, and these two parts to be folded together, the line FG forming the fold; then the point A would fall upon the point B, the point C upon the point H, and the point D upon the point E; otherwise, the polygon is not a regular polygon, nor the circumscribed square a perfect square. In a similar manner, it may be demonstrated that the line AD is equal to DC, by supposing the figure to be folded upon the line DL.

from O, the apex of the roof, upon the plane or level of the plates CA, AB, &c.

Then, in the right-angled triangle O'FA, the sum of the squares of the two sides AF and FO' will equal the square of the hypotenuse AO'

Having found above that FG=38 ft. 7.52 in., then FO' will equal half this number, or 19 ft. 3.76 in., or 231.76 inches, the square of which is 53,712.6976 inches.

FA is half of the given side AB, and is 8 feet, or 96 inches, of which the square is 9,216 inches, which, being added to 53,712.6976 inches, is 62,928.6976 inches, the square root of which is 250.85 inches, or 20 ft. 10.85 in., the length of AO', or half the diagonal width of the building. Double this number is 41 ft. 9.70 in., the length of AP, the *diagonal width required.*

Half the diagonal width is of course the run of the hip rafters, and half the square width is the run of the middle jack rafters; and, having ascertained these, the lengths of the rafters are calculated according to the rule given at the commencement of this general explanation of the Tables—by taking the square root of the sum of the squares of the *run* and the *rise* of any given rafter.

II. Width of Octagon given to find the Diagonal and the Side.

It sometimes happens, as in church spires for example, that the width of an octagon is given, from which the other dimensions must be found.

Let PC, the width of a regular octagon, be given, to find AB the side, and AE the diagonal.

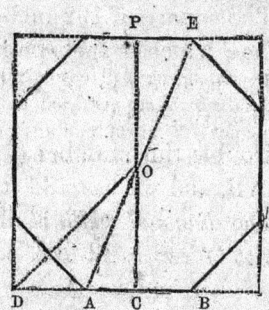

Draw OD from the centre of the octagon to an angle of the circumscribed square. Then $OD^2 = CD^2 + OC^2$, or $2OC^2$, since OD is the hypotenuse of the triangle ODC, of which the other two sides OC and DC are equal to each other, and each one equals half the given width of the octagon. Then, since OA bisects the vertical angle of the triangle COD, it divides the base into two segments, which are proportional to the adjacent sides (Part I., Prop. XXVI.); and we have the following proportion:

$$DO : OC :: DA : AC;$$

and, by composition,
$$DO+OC : OC :: DA+AC : AC;$$
but AC is half the required side AB.

Having obtained, by the above formula, the length of AC, it will be easy to obtain that of OA, since $OA^2 = OC^2 + AC^2$.

Example. Suppose PC, the given width, equals 10 ft. 8 in., which is the width of the base of the church spire described in Plate 28. Reducing this number to inches, to insure greater accuracy, we have PC=128 inches. And OD would then equal the square root of the sum of the squares of OC and DC, each of which equals 64 inches. Double the square of 64 inches equals 8192 inches, the square root of which is 90.51 inches, which is the length of OD; then, by applying or substituting this value in the first proportion given above, we have
$$90.51 \text{ in.} : 64 \text{ in.} :: DA : AC;$$
and DA being yet unknown, we ascertain it by composition, thus:
$$90.51+64 : 64 :: DA+AC, \text{ or } DC : AC;$$
or,
$$154.51 : 64 :: 64 : AC.$$
Multiplying the middle terms of this proportion together, and dividing the product by the first term, we have the value of the last term, or AC, equal to 26.51 inches. Double this, and we have AB, *the required side, equal to 53.02 inches, or 4 ft. 5.02 in.*, and $OC^2 + AC^2 = AO^2$, or $702.78 + 4096 = 4798.78$ inches, the square root of which is 69.27 inches, or 5 ft. 9.27 in.; and the whole of the *required diagonal* equals twice this number, or 11 ft. 6.54 in.

Note.—Since all regular octagons are similar figures, any two regular octagons of different dimensions will not only have their sides proportional, but their widths and their diagonal widths proportional also; and if we have the exact dimensions of all the parts of one octagon given, and any one part of the other octagon also given, then all its remaining parts can be found by proportion.

Example 1. Required the diagonal width of a regular octagon, the side of which is 12 feet.

Let us compare this with another octagon, all the dimensions of which we know, or which we can find from the Table; say, an octagon of 16 feet side, the diagonal width of which, as given in the Table, is

EXPLANATION OF TABLES.

41 ft. 9.7 in.; then, since all the parts of the one figure are proportional to the corresponding parts of the other, we shall have

side to side, as diagonal width to diagonal width;

or,   16 : 12 : : 41 9.7 to the answer = 31 ft. 4.27 in.,

Thus:

We multiply the second and third terms together, and divide by the first:

```
    41 ft. 9.7 in.
       12
      ───
      492
        9.7
      ─────
   16)501.7(31.356 feet and decimals of a foot, which we reduce to
      48             feet and inches, thus:
      ──
      21                      31.356
      16                          12
      ──                      ──────
      57                       4.272
      48
      ──
      90
      80
      ──
      100
```

By multiplying the tenths of a foot by 12 to bring them to inches, and disregarding the third decimal figure, we have for a final answer 31 ft. $4\frac{27}{100}$ in. as the required answer; which is verified by the number as given in the Table.

Example 2. Required the *side* of a regular octagon, the square width of which is 30 feet. We compare this with the same octagon as before, and have

width to width as side to side;

or,   38 7.52 : 30 : : 16 : to the answer = 12 feet 5.12 inches,

Thus:

as in this case the first term or divisor is a compound number, we reduce all the three given terms to inches, and have

38 ft. 7.52 in. = 463.52 inches,
30 feet = 360 inches,
16 feet = 192 inches.

CARPENTRY MADE EASY.

So that the proportion, in inches, is
$$463.52 : 360 :: 192 : \text{answer} = 12 \text{ ft. } 5.12 \text{ in.}$$

```
              360
             -----
             11520
              576
      463.52)69120(149.119 in., or 12 ft. 5.12 in., Ans.
             46352
             ------
             227680
             185408
             ------
              422720
              417168
              ------
                55520
                46352
                -----
                 91680
                 46352
                 -----
                 453280
```

TABLE III.

OCTAGONAL ROOFS.—One side of the Octagon being given to find: 1. The Width of the Building. 2. Its Diagonal Width. 3. The Length of the Hip Rafters. 4. The Length of the Middle Jack Rafters, in Feet, Inches, and Hundredths of an Inch. Rise of the Roof to the Foot on the Jack Rafters.

Length of One Side.	Width of Building.	Diagonal Width of Building.	1 inch Rise.		2 inch Rise.		3 inch Rise.		4 inch Rise.		5 inch Rise.		6 inch Rise.	
			Jack.	Hip.	Jack.	Hip.	Jack.	Hip.	Jack.	Hip.	Jack.	Hip.	Jack.	Hip.
6 ft.	14 : 5.82	16 : 8.14	7 : 3.21	7 : 10.35	7 : 4.11	7 : 11.18	7 : 5.59	8 : 0.55	7 : 7.61	8 : 2.43	7 : 10.15	8 : 4.79	8 : 1.17	8 : 7.62
7 "	16 : 10.79	18 : 3.49	8 : 5.75	9 : 2.07	8 : 6.79	9 : 3.04	8 : 8.49	9 : 4.63	8 : 10.87	9 : 6.83	9 : 1.81	9 : 9.69	9 : 5.36	10 : 0.89
8 "	19 : 3.76	20 : 10.86	9 : 8.28	10 : 5.80	9 : 9.47	10 : 6.90	9 : 11.42	10 : 8.72	10 : 2.14	10 : 11.24	10 : 6.53	11 : 2.38	10 : 9.56	11 : 6.16
9 "	21 : 8.73	23 : 6.20	10 : 10.81	11 : 9.53	11 : 0.16	11 : 10.76	11 : 2.35	12 : 0.81	11 : 5.41	12 : 3.64	11 : 9.22	12 : 7.18	12 : 1.75	12 : 11.43
10 "	24 : 1.70	26 : 1.56	12 : 1.35	13 : 1.25	12 : 2.84	13 : 2.62	12 : 5.28	13 : 4.90	12 : 8.68	13 : 8.05	13 : 0.91	13 : 11.98	13 : 6.95	14 : 4.70
11 "	26 : 6.67	28 : 8.92	13 : 3.88	14 : 4.98	13 : 5.52	14 : 6.68	13 : 8.21	14 : 9	13 : 11.95	15 : 0.45	14 : 4.60	15 : 4.78	14 : 10.14	15 : 9.97
12 "	28 : 11.64	31 : 4.27	14 : 6.42	15 : 8.70	14 : 8.21	15 : 10.35	14 : 11.14	16 : 1.09	15 : 3.23	16 : 4.86	15 : 8.30	16 : 9.68	16 : 2.34	17 : 3.24
14 "	33 : 9.58	36 : 6.98	16 : 11.60	18 : 4.15	17 : 1.58	18 : 6.07	17 : 5	18 : 9.27	17 : 9.76	19 : 1.67	18 : 3.68	19 : 7.17	18 : 10.73	20 : 1.78
16 "	38 : 7.52	41 : 9.70	19 : 4.68	20 : 11.60	19 : 6.95	21 : 1.80	19 : 10.85	21 : 5.45	20 : 4.29	21 : 10.48	20 : 11.06	22 : 4.77	21 : 7.12	23 : 0.32
18 "	43 : 5.46	47 : 0.42	21 : 9.63	23 : 7.05	22 : 0.32	23 : 9.62	22 : 4.70	24 : 1.63	22 : 10.83	24 : 7.29	23 : 6.45	25 : 2.37	24 : 3.51	25 : 10.86
20 "	48 : 3.40	52 : 3.12	24 : 2.70	26 : 2.50	24 : 5.68	26 : 5.25	24 : 10.56	26 : 9.81	25 : 5.36	27 : 4.10	26 : 1.83	27 : 11.96	26 : 11.90	28 : 9.40
22 "	53 : 1.34	57 : 5.83	26 : 7.77	28 : 9.95	26 : 11.05	29 : 0.97	27 : 4.42	29 : 6	27 : 11.90	30 : 0.91	28 : 9.21	30 : 9.56	29 : 8.29	31 : 7.94
24 "	57 : 11.28	62 : 8.55	29 : 0.84	31 : 5.40	29 : 4.42	31 : 8.70	29 : 10.27	32 : 2.17	30 : 6.44	32 : 9.72	31 : 4.60	33 : 7.16	32 : 4.68	34 : 6.48
26 "	62 : 9.22	67 : 11.26	31 : 5.91	34 : 0.85	31 : 9.79	34 : 4.42	32 : 4.13	34 : 10.35	33 : 0.97	35 : 6.53	33 : 11.98	36 : 4.75	35 : 1.07	37 : 5.02
28 "	67 : 7.16	73 : 1.97	33 : 10.98	36 : 8.30	34 : 3.16	37 : 0.15	34 : 10	37 : 6.63	35 : 7.51	38 : 3.34	36 : 7.36	39 : 2.35	37 : 9.46	40 : 3.56
30 "	72 : 5.10	78 : 4.68	36 : 4.05	39 : 3.75	36 : 8.53	39 : 7.87	37 : 3.84	40 : 2.72	38 : 2.05	41 : 0.14	39 : 2.75	41 : 11.75	40 : 5.85	43 : 2.10

TABLE IV.

The *length of braces*, like the length of rafters, must be determined by extracting the square root of the sum of the squares of the perpendicular and the horizontal runs.

This table embraces almost every length that can be required in framing buildings, and comprises those of both regular and irregular runs.

The exact length is here given to the hundredth part of an inch; but *practically* it will be found best to cut each brace from a sixteenth to an eighth of an inch longer than the exact rule requires, in order to compensate for compression and the shrinkage of the timber.

TABLE IV.

Length of Braces given in Feet, Inches, and Hundredths of an Inch.

Length of Run.	Length of Brace.	Length of Run.	Length of Brace.	Length of Run.	Length of Brace.
Ft. In. Ft. In.		Ft. In. Ft. In.		Ft. In. Ft. In.	
0 : 6 by 0 : 6	0 : 8.48	3 : 3 by 3 : 3	4 : 7.15	5 : 6 by 5 : 6	7 : 9.33
0 : 6 by 0 : 9	0 : 10.81	3 : 3 by 3 : 6	4 : 9.31	5 : 9 by 5 : 9	8 : 1.58
0 : 9 by 0 : 9	1 : 0.72	3 : 3 by 3 : 9	4 : 11.54	6 : 0 by 6 : 0	8 : 5.82
0 : 9 by 1 : 0	1 : 3	3 : 3 by 4 : 0	5 : 1.84	6 : 3 by 6 : 3	8 : 10.06
1 : 0 by 1 : 0	1 : 4.97	3 : 6 by 3 : 6	4 : 11.39	6 : 6 by 6 : 6	9 : 2.30
1 : 0 by 1 : 3	1 : 7.20	3 : 6 by 3 : 9	5 : 1.55	6 : 9 by 6 : 9	9 : 6.55
1 : 3 by 1 : 3	1 : 9.23	3 : 6 by 4 : 0	5 : 3.78	7 : 0 by 7 : 0	9 : 10.79
1 : 3 by 1 : 6	1 : 11.43	3 : 9 by 3 : 9	5 : 3.63	7 : 3 by 7 : 3	10 : 3.03
1 : 6 by 1 : 6	2 : 1.45	3 : 9 by 4 : 0	5 : 5.79	7 : 6 by 7 : 6	10 : 7 28
1 : 6 by 1 : 9	2 : 3.65	4 : 0 by 4 : 0	5 : 7.88	7 : 9 by 7 : 9	10 : 11.52
1 : 9 by 1 : 9	2 : 5.69	4 : 0 by 4 : 3	5 : 10.03	8 : 0 by 8 : 0	11 : 3.76
1 : 9 by 2 : 0	2 : 7.89	4 : 0 by 4 : 6	6 : 0.25	8 : 3 by 8 : 3	11 : 8
2 : 0 by 2 : 0	2 : 9.94	4 : 0 by 4 : 9	6 : 2.51	8 : 6 by 8 : 6	12 : 0.24
2 : 0 by 2 : 3	3 : 0.12	4 : 0 by 5 : 0	6 : 4.83	8 : 9 by 8 : 9	12 : 4.49
2 : 0 by 2 : 6	3 : 2.41	4 : 3 by 4 : 3	6 : 0.12	9 : 0 by 9 : 0	12 : 8.73
2 : 3 by 2 : 6	3 : 4.36	4 : 3 by 4 : 6	6 : 2.27	9 : 6 by 9 : 6	13 : 5.22
2 : 6 by 2 : 6	3 : 6.42	4 : 3 by 4 : 9	6 : 4.49	10 : 0 by 10 : 0	14 : 1.70
2 : 6 by 2 : 9	3 : 8.59	4 : 3 by 5 : 0	6 : 6.74	10 : 6 by 10 : 6	14 : 10.19
2 : 9 by 2 : 9	3 : 10.66	4 : 6 by 4 : 6	6 : 4.36	11 : 0 by 11 : 0	15 : 6.67
2 : 9 by 3 : 0	4 : 0.83	4 : 6 by 4 : 9	6 : 6.51	11 : 6 by 11 : 6	16 : 3.16
3 : 0 by 3 : 0	4 : 2.91	4 : 6 by 5 : 0	6 : 8.72	12 : 0 by 12 : 0	16 : 11.64
3 : 0 by 3 : 3	4 : 5.02	4 : 9 by 4 : 9	6 : 8.61	12 : 6 by 12 : 6	17 : 8.13
3 : 0 by 3 : 6	4 : 7.31	4 : 9 by 5 : 0	6 : 10.75	13 : 0 by 13 : 0	18 : 4.61
3 : 0 by 3 : 9	4 : 9.62	5 : 0 by 5 : 0	7 : 0.85	13 : 6 by 13 : 6	19 : 1.10
3 : 0 by 4 : 0	5 :	5 : 3 by 5 : 3	7 : 5.09	14 : 0 by 14 : 0	19 : 9.58

TABLE V.

Weight of Square Iron in Pounds and Ounces.

Size. Inches.	1 foot. lbs. oz.	2 feet. lbs. oz.	3 feet. lbs. oz.	4 feet. lbs. oz.	5 feet. lbs. oz.	6 feet. lbs. oz.	7 feet. lbs. oz.	8 feet. lbs. oz.	9 feet. lbs. oz.
½	0 : 13	1 : 11	2 : 8	2 : 6	4 : 3	5 : 2	5 : 15	6 : 13	7 : 10
⅝	1 : 5	2 : 10	4 : 0	5 : 5	6 : 10	7 : 9	9 : 5	10 : 10	12 : 0
¾	1 : 15	3 : 14	5 : 13	7 : 12	9 : 10	11 : 9	13 : 7	15 : 6	17 : 4
⅞	2 : 10	5 : 4	7 : 14	10 : 8	13 : 0	15 : 8	18 : 2	20 : 12	23 : 6
1	3 : 6	6 : 12	10 : 2	13 : 5	16 : 12	20 : 4	23 : 10	27 : 0	30 : 6
1⅛	4 : 5	8 : 10	12 : 15	17 : 3	21 : 8	25 : 12	30 : 0	34 : 5	38 : 9
1¼	5 : 5	10 : 10	15 : 15	21 : 2	26 : 7	31 : 12	37 : 0	42 : 4	47 : 8
1⅜	6 : 6	12 : 12	19 : 3	25 : 9	32 : 0	38 : 6	44 : 12	51 : 2	57 : 8
1½	7 : 10	15 : 4	22 : 12	30 : 6	38 : 0	45 : 10	53 : 4	60 : 14	68 : 7
1⅝	8 : 14	17 : 12	26 : 11	35 : 9	44 : 8	53 : 7	62 : 6	71 : 5	80 : 4
1¾	10 : 6	20 : 12	31 : 2	41 : 7	51 : 13	62 : 2	72 : 8	82 : 14	93 : 4
1⅞	11 : 14	23 : 12	35 : 10	47 : 8	59 : 6	71 : 5	83 : 3	95 : 2	107 : 0
2	13 : 8	27 : 0	40 : 10	54 : 2	67 : 10	81 : 2	94 : 10	102 : 03	121 : 11
2⅛	15 : 5	30 : 8	45 : 13	61 : 2	76 : 6	91 : 10	106 : 13	122 : 2	137 : 6
2¼	17 : 2	34 : 3	51 : 5	68 : 6	85 : 9	102 : 11	119 : 13	136 : 15	154 : 0
2⅜	19 : 1	38 : 2	57 : 3	76 : 4	95 : 5	114 : 6	133 : 7	152 : 8	171 : 9
2½	21 : 1	42 : 3	63 : 6	84 : 8	105 : 10	126 : 14	147 : 15	169 : 0	190 : 1
2⅝	23 : 5	46 : 10	69 : 15	93 : 3	116 : 8	139 : 13	163 : 1	186 : 5	209 : 10
2¾	25 : 10	51 : 02	76 : 12	102 : 3	127 : 13	153 : 6	178 : 15	204 : 8	230 : 0
2⅞	27 : 14	55 : 14	83 : 13	111 : 12	139 : 11	167 : 10	195 : 9	223 : 8	251 : 7
3	30 : 6	60 : 12	91 : 3	121 : 9	152 : 2	182 : 8	212 : 14	243 : 5	273 : 11
3⅛	33 : 0	66 : 0	99 : 0	132 : 0	165 : 1	198 : 1	231 : 1	264 : 2	297 : 2
3¼	35 : 11	71 : 6	107 : 2	142 : 13	178 : 8	214 : 3	249 : 15	285 : 10	321 : 5
3⅜	38 : 8	77 : 0	115 : 8	154 : 0	192 : 8	231 : 0	269 : 8	308 : 0	346 : 8
3½	41 : 6	82 : 12	124 : 3	167 : 9	207 : 0	248 : 6	289 : 12	331 : 3	372 : 10
3⅝	44 : 6	88 : 12	133 : 4	177 : 11	221 : 2	266 : 8	310 : 14	355 : 5	399 : 13
3¾	47 : 8	95 : 1	142 : 9	190 : 2	237 : 11	285 : 3	332 : 11	380 : 5	427 : 13
3⅞	50 : 13	101 : 8	152 : 5	203 : 0	253 : 13	304 : 8	355 : 5	406 : 0	456 : 13
4	54 : 2	108 : 3	162 : 4	216 : 5	270 : 6	324 : 8	376 : 10	432 : 11	486 : 13
4⅛	57 : 8	115 : 0	172 : 10	230 : 2	287 : 10	345 : 2	402 : 10	460 : 2	517 : 11
4¼	61 : 1	122 : 2	183 : 3	244 : 4	305 : 5	366 : 6	427 : 7	488 : 7	549 : 8
4⅜	64 : 11	129 : 6	194 : 2	258 : 13	323 : 8	388 : 3	452 : 14	517 : 10	582 : 5
4½	68 : 6	136 : 14	205 : 5	273 : 13	342 : 3	410 : 11	479 : 2	547 : 10	616 : 0
4⅝	72 : 5	144 : 10	216 : 15	289 : 3	361 : 8	433 : 13	506 : 2	578 : 7	450 : 11
4¾	76 : 5	152 : 8	228 : 12	305 : 1	381 : 5	457 : 9	533 : 13	610 : 1	686 : 6
4⅞	80 : 5	160 : 11	241 : 0	221 : 5	401 : 11	482 : 0	562 : 5	642 : 11	723 : 0
5	84 : 8	169 : 0	253 : 6	337 : 15	422 : 6	506 : 15	591 : 6	675 : 14	760 : 5

EXPLANATION OF TABLES.

TABLE V.—*Continued.*

Weight of Square Iron in Pounds and Ounces.

Size.	10 feet.	11 feet.	12 feet.	13 feet.	14 feet.	15 feet.	16 feet.	17 feet.	18 feet.
Inches.	lbs. oz.	lbs. oz.	lbs. oz.	lbs. oz.	lbs. oz.	lbs. oz.	lbs. oz.	lbs. oz.	lbs. oz.
½	8 : 8	9 : 5	10 : 2	11 : 0	11 : 13	12 : 9	13 : 8	14 : 6	15 : 3
⅝	13 : 5	14 : 10	16 : 0	17 : 5	18 : 10	19 : 15	21 : 4	22 : 9	23 : 14
¾	19 : 0	20 : 15	22 : 13	24 : 12	26 : 10	28 : 8	30 : 6	32 : 4	34 : 02
⅞	26 : 0	28 : 8	31 : 2	33 : 12	36 : 6	38 : 14	41 : 8	44 : 2	46 : 11
1	33 : 12	37 : 3	40 : 10	44 : 0	47 : 6	50 : 12	54 : 2	57 : 8	60 : 14
1⅛	42 : 14	47 : 2	51 : 6	55 : 11	59 : 15	64 : 4	68 : 8	72 : 13	77 : 0
1¼	52 : 12	58 : 1	63 : 6	68 : 11	74 : 0	79 : 4	84 : 8	89 : 13	95 : 0
1⅜	63 : 14	70 : 4	76 : 10	83 : 0	89 : 7	95 : 14	102 : 2	108 : 9	115 : 0
1½	76 : 0	83 : 10	91 : 4	98 : 14	106 : 8	114 : 2	121 : 12	129 : 6	137 : 0
1⅝	89 : 4	98 : 3	107 : 2	116 : 1	125 : 0	133 : 15	142 : 14	151 : 13	160 : 11
1¾	103 : 10	114 : 0	124 : 5	134 : 11	145 : 0	155 : 5	165 : 11	176 : 0	186 : 6
1⅞	118 : 13	130 : 11	142 : 10	154 : 8	166 : 6	178 : 3	190 : 2	202 : 0	213 : 14
2	135 : 3	148 : 11	162 : 3	175 : 12	189 : 4	202 : 13	216 : 5	229 : 13	243 : 6
2⅛	152 : 10	167 : 14	183 : 3	198 : 7	213 : 11	229 : 0	244 : 5	259 : 9	274 : 14
2¼	171 : 2	188 : 8	205 : 5	222 : 8	239 : 10	256 : 11	273 : 13	290 : 15	308 : 0
2⅜	190 : 10	209 : 11	228 : 12	247 : 14	266 : 15	286 : 0	305 : 1	324 : 2	343 : 3
2½	211 : 3	232 : 5	253 : 7	274 : 9	295 : 12	316 : 14	337 : 15	359 : 0	380 : 3
2⅝	232 : 15	256 : 3	279 : 8	302 : 13	326 : 2	349 : 7	372 : 12	396 : 0	419 : 5
2¾	255 : 10	281 : 3	306 : 13	332 : 6	357 : 13	383 : 6	409 :	434 : 8	460 : 1
2⅞	279 : 6	307 : 5	335 : 4	363 : 3	391 : 1	419 : 0	447 : 0	475 : 0	502 : 14
3	304 : 2	334 : 9	365 : 0	395 : 6	425 : 13	456 : 3	486 : 10	517 : 1	547 : 8
3⅛	330 : 2	363 : 2	396 : 2	329 : 2	462 : 2	495 : 3	528 : 3	561 : 3	594 : 3
3¼	357 : 0	392 : 11	428 : 6	464 : 3	500 : 0	535 : 11	571 : 5	607 : 0	642 : 11
3⅜	385 : 0	423 : 8	462 : 0	500 : 8	539 : 0	577 : 8	616 : 0	654 : 9	693 : 1
3½	414 : 1	455 : 8	496 : 15	538 : 5	579 : 11	621 : 2	662 : 8	703 : 14	745 : 5
3⅝	444 : 3	488 : 9	533 : 0	577 : 6	621 : 15	666 : 5	710 : 11	755 : 2	799 : 8
3¾	475 : 5	522 : 14	570 : 6	617 : 15	665 : 8	713 : 0	760 : 8	808 : 1	855 : 10
3⅞	507 : 10	558 : 5	609 : 1	659 : 13	710 : 10	761 : 5	812 : 2	862 : 15	913 : 10
4	540 : 14	594 : 15	649 : 0	703 : 2	757 : 3	811 : 4	865 : 5	919 : 0	973 : 8
4⅛	575 : 3	632 : 11	690 : 3	747 : 11	805 : 3	862 : 12	920 : 5	977 : 13	1035 : 5
4¼	610 : 9	671 : 10	732 : 11	793 : 12	854 : 13	915 : 14	976 : 15	1037 : 15	1099 : 0
4⅜	646 : 0	711 : 11	776 : 6	841 : 2	905 : 13	970 : 8	1035 : 3	1099 : 14	1164 : 10
4½	684 : 8	752 : 15	821 : 6	889 : 13	958 : 5	1026 : 11	1095 : 3	1163 : 10	1232 : 2
4⅝	721 : 1	795 : 6	867 : 11	940 : 0	1012 : 5	1084 : 10	1156 : 15	1229 : 3	1301 : 8
4¾	762 : 10	838 : 15	915 : 3	991 : 7	1067 : 11	1144 : 0	1220 : 3	1296 : 8	1372 : 13
4⅞	803 : 5	883 : 11	964 : 0	1044 : 5	1124 : 11	1205 : 0	1285 : 5	1365 : 11	1446 : 0
5	844 : 13	929 : 5	1013 : 14	1098 : 3	1182 : 11	1267 : 3	1351 : 11	1436 : 3	1520 : 10

TABLE VI.

Weight of Flat Iron in Pounds and Ounces.

Thick. Inches.	Wide. Inches.	1 foot. lbs. oz.	2 feet. lbs. oz.	3 feet. lbs. oz.	4 feet. lbs. oz.	5 feet. lbs. oz.	6 feet. lbs. oz.	7 feet. lbs. oz.	8 feet. lbs. oz.	9 feet. lbs. oz.	10 feet. lbs. oz.
¼	1	0:13	1:11	2: 8	3: 6	4: 2	5: 0	5:14	6:13	7:10	8: 8
	1¼	1: 1	2: 2	3: 3	4: 3	5: 4	6: 5	7: 6	8: 7	9: 8	10: 9
	1½	1: 4	2: 8	3:12	5: 1	6: 5	7: 9	8:13	10: 1	11: 5	12:10
	1¾	1: 8	3: 0	4: 7	5:14	7: 6	8:14	10: 6	11:13	13: 5	14:13
	2	1:11	3: 6	5: 1	6:13	8: 8	10: 1	11:13	13: 8	15: 3	16:14
	2¼	1:14	3:12	5:11	7:10	9: 8	11: 6	13: 4	15: 3	17: 1	19: 0
	2½	2: 1	4: 3	6: 5	8: 7	10: 9	12:11	14:13	16:14	19: 0	21: 1
	2¾	2: 5	4:10	7: 0	9: 5	11:10	13:14	16: 5	18:10	20:15	22: 3
	3	2: 8	5: 1	7:10	10: 1	12:11	15: 3	17:11	20: 5	22:13	25: 5
	3¼	2:12	5: 8	8: 3	11: 0	13:12	16: 8	19: 3	22: 0	24:12	27: 8
	3½	3: 0	5:14	8:13	11:12	14:11	17:10	20:10	23: 9	26: 9	29: 8
	3¾	3: 3	6: 5	9: 8	12:11	15:13	19: 0	22: 3	25: 6	28: 8	31:11
	4	3: 6	6:13	10: 2	13: 8	16:14	20: 5	23:11	27: 0	30: 6	33:13
⅜	1	1: 4	2: 8	3:12	5: 1	6: 5	7: 9	8:14	10: 2	11: 6	12:11
	1¼	1:10	3: 4	4:13	6: 5	7:14	9: 8	11: 1	12:11	14: 5	15:13
	1½	1:14	3:12	5:11	7:10	9: 8	11: 6	13: 5	15: 2	17: 1	19: 0
	1¾	2: 3	4: 6	6:10	8:14	11: 1	13: 5	15: 8	17:11	20: 1	22: 3
	2	2: 8	5: 1	7: 9	10: 1	12: 9	15: 2	17:11	20: 5	22:11	25: 6
	2¼	2:14	5:11	8: 8	11: 6	14: 4	17: 2	20: 0	22:12	25:10	28: 8
	2½	3: 3	6: 6	9: 8	12:11	15:13	19: 0	22: 3	25: 6	28: 8	31:11
	2¾	3: 8	7: 0	10: 8	13:15	17: 7	20:14	24: 7	27:15	31: 7	34:15
	3	3:13	7:10	11: 6	15: 3	19: 0	22:12	26: 9	30: 6	34: 3	38: 0
	3¼	4: 2	8: 4	12: 6	16: 8	20:10	24:12	28:14	33: 0	37: 2	41: 4
	3½	4: 7	8:14	13: 5	17:12	22: 3	26:10	31: 0	35: 7	39:15	44: 6
	3¾	4:12	9: 8	14: 4	19: 0	23:12	28: 8	33: 4	38: 0	42:12	47: 8
	4	5: 1	10: 2	15: 3	20: 4	25: 5	30: 6	35: 8	40: 9	45:10	50:11
½	1	1:11	3: 6	5: 1	6:13	8: 8	10: 2	11:13	13: 8	15: 3	16:14
	1¼	2: 1	4: 3	6: 5	8: 7	10: 9	12:11	14:13	16:14	19: 0	21: 2
	1½	2: 8	5: 1	7: 9	10: 1	12:10	15: 3	17:11	20: 5	22:13	25: 5
	1¾	3: 0	5:15	8:14	11:13	14:12	17:11	20:10	23:10	26: 9	29: 9
	2	3: 6	6:12	10: 2	13: 8	16:14	20: 5	23:10	27: 0	30: 6	33:12
	2¼	3:13	7:10	11: 7	15: 3	19: 0	22:13	26:10	30: 7	34: 4	38: 0
	2½	4: 3	8: 6	12:10	16:14	21: 2	25: 5	26: 9	33:14	38: 2	42: 4
	2¾	4:10	9: 5	13:15	18: 9	23: 3	27:14	32: 8	37: 3	41:13	46: 8
	3	5: 1	10: 2	15: 3	20: 4	25: 5	30: 6	35: 8	40: 9	45:10	50:11
	3¼	5: 8	11: 0	16: 8	22: 0	27: 8	33: 0	38: 8	44: 0	49: 8	55: 0
	3½	5:14	11:12	17:11	23:10	29: 9	35: 8	41: 7	47: 5	53: 4	59: 3

EXPLANATION OF TABLES.

TABLE VI.—Continued.

Weight of Flat Iron in Pounds and Ounces.

Thick. Inches.	Wide. Inches.	1 foot. lbs. oz.	2 feet. lbs. oz.	3 feet. lbs. oz.	4 feet. lbs. oz.	5 feet. lbs. oz.	6 feet. lbs. oz.	7 feet. lbs. oz.	8 feet. lbs. oz.	9 feet. lbs. oz.	10 feet. lbs. oz.
½	3¾	6: 5	12:11	19: 0	25: 5	31:11	38: 0	44: 6	50:11	57: 0	63: 5
	4	6:12	13: 8	20: 5	27: 0	33:12	40: 9	47: 4	54: 0	60:12	67: 9
⅝	1	2: 1	4: 3	6: 5	8: 7	10: 9	12:11	14:13	16:15	19: 0	21: 2
	1¼	2:10	5: 5	7:15	10: 9	13: 3	15:13	18: 8	21: 2	23:12	26: 6
	1½	3: 3	6: 6	9: 8	12:11	15:13	19: 0	22: 3	25: 6	28: 8	31:11
	1¾	3:11	7: 6	11: 1	14:13	18: 8	22: 3	25:14	29: 9	33: 4	37: 0
	2	4: 3	8: 6	12:10	16:14	21: 1	25: 5	29: 9	33:12	38: 0	42: 3
	2¼	4:12	9: 8	14: 5	19: 0	23:12	28: 8	33: 5	38: 0	42:12	47: 8
	2½	5: 5	10: 9	15:13	21: 1	26: 6	31:10	37: 0	42: 3	47: 8	52:12
	2¾	5:13	11:10	17: 6	23: 3	29: 0	34:13	40:11	46: 8	52: 5	58: 2
	3	6: 5	12:11	19: 0	25: 5	31:11	38: 0	44: 6	50:11	57:10	63: 0
	3¼	6:14	13:12	20: 9	27: 8	34: 5	41: 3	48: 1	55: 0	61:12	68:10
	3½	7: 6	14:12	22: 3	29: 9	37: 0	44: 6	51:13	59: 3	66: 8	73:14
	3¾	7:14	15:12	23:11	31:10	39: 9	47: 8	55: 7	63: 6	71: 5	79: 4
	4	8: 7	16:14	25: 5	33:12	42: 3	50:10	59: 1	67: 9	76: 0	84: 8
¾	1	2: 8	5: 1	7: 9	10: 1	12:10	15: 3	17:11	20: 5	22:13	25: 5
	1¼	3: 3	6: 6	9: 8	12:10	15:13	19: 0	22: 3	25: 6	28: 8	31:11
	1½	3:12	7: 9	11: 6	15: 3	19: 0	22:12	26: 9	30: 6	34: 3	38: 0
	1¾	4: 7	8:14	13: 5	17:12	22: 3	26:10	31: 1	35: 8	39:15	44: 6
	2	5: 1	10: 2	15: 3	20: 4	25: 5	30: 6	35: 8	40: 9	45:10	50:11
	2¼	5:11	11: 6	17: 1	22:12	28: 8	34: 3	39:15	45:10	51: 5	57: 0
	2½	6: 5	12:10	19: 0	25: 5	31:10	38: 0	44: 6	50:11	57: 0	63: 5
	2¾	7: 0	14: 0	21: 0	28: 0	35: 0	42: 0	49: 0	56: 0	63: 0	69: 0
	3	7:10	15: 4	22:13	30: 6	38: 0	45:10	53: 4	60:14	68: 8	76: 0
	3¼	8: 4	16: 8	24:12	33: 0	41: 4	49: 7	57:12	66: 0	74: 3	82: 7
	3½	8:14	17:12	26:10	35: 8	44: 6	53: 4	62: 6	71: 0	79:14	88:12
	3¾	9: 8	19: 0	28: 8	38: 0	47: 8	57: 0	66: 8	76: 0	85: 8	95: 0
	4	10: 2	20: 4	30: 6	40: 9	50:11	60:14	70:15	81: 1	91: 3	101: 6
1	1½	5: 1	10: 2	15: 3	20: 4	25: 5	30: 6	35: 8	40: 9	45:10	50:11
	2	6:12	13: 8	20: 4	27: 0	33:12	40: 0	47: 5	54: 0	60:12	67: 9
	3	10: 2	20: 4	30: 6	40: 9	50:11	60:13	70:15	81: 1	91: 3	101: 5
	4	13: 8	27: 0	40: 9	54: 1	67: 9	81: 1	94: 9	108: 1	121:10	135: 2
	5	16:14	33:12	50:11	67: 9	84: 8	101: 6	118: 5	135: 4	152: 2	169: 0
	6	20: 5	40:10	60:15	81: 2	101: 6	121:11	141:14	162: 3	182: 8	202:12

CARPENTRY MADE EASY.

TABLE VII.

Weight of Round Iron in Pounds and Ounces.

Size. Diameter in inches.	1 foot. lbs. oz.	2 feet. lbs. oz.	3 feet. lbs. oz.	4 feet. lbs. oz.	5 feet. lbs. oz.	6 feet. lbs. oz.	7 feet. lbs. oz.	8 feet. lbs. oz.	9 feet. lbs. oz.
½	0:11	1:5	2:0	2:11	3:5	4:0	4:11	5:5	6:0
⅝	1:0	2:1	3:2	4:3	5:4	6:5	7:5	8:6	9:7
¾	1:8	3:0	4:8	6:0	7:8	9:0	10:8	12:0	13:8
⅞	2:0	4:1	6:1	8:2	10:3	12:3	14:4	16:5	18:5
1	2:11	5:5	8:0	10:10	13:5	15:15	18:10	21:3	23:14
1⅛	3:6	6:12	10:2	13:7	16:13	20:3	23:8	26:14	30:4
1¼	4:3	8:6	12:8	16:11	20:14	25:0	29:3	33:6	37:8
1⅜	5:0	10:0	15:1	20:1	25:2	30:2	35:2	40:3	45:3
1½	6:0	11:15	17:15	23:14	29:14	35:13	41:12	47:12	53:11
1⅝	7:0	14:0	21:0	28:0	35:1	42:1	49:1	56:1	63:1
1¾	8:2	16:4	24:6	32:8	40:10	48:12	56:14	65:0	72:3
1⅞	9:5	18:11	28:	37:5	46:11	56:0	65:5	74:11	84:0
2	10:10	21:4	31:14	42:8	53:2	63:12	74:5	84:14	95:8
2⅛	12:	24:	36:	48:	60:	72:	84:	96:	108:
2¼	13:8	26:14	40:6	53:13	67:4	80:9	94:2	107:8	121:
2⅜	15:	30:	45:	60:	75:	89:15	104:13	119:13	134:13
2½	16:11	33:4	50:1	66:12	83:7	100:1	116:12	133:8	150:3
2⅝	18:13	37:10	54:6	73:3	92:10	112:8	131:4	150:0	168:12
2¾	20:1	40:3	60:5	80:6	100:7	120:8	140:9	160:10	180:11
2⅞	21:15	43:14	65:13	87:12	109:11	131:10	153:9	175:8	197:7
3	23:14	47:12	71:11	95:9	119:7	143:5	167:3	191:1	215:0
3⅛	25:14	51:13	77:12	103:11	129:10	155:9	181:8	207:7	233:6
3¼	28:0	56:1	84:2	112:3	140:3	168:4	196:5	224:5	253:6
3⅜	30:4	60:5	90:12	121:0	151:4	181:7	211:11	241:15	272:3
3½	32:8	65:0	97:8	130:0	162:9	195:1	127:9	260:1	292:9
3⅝	34:14	69:12	104:10	139:8	174:6	209:5	244:3	279:1	314:0
3¾	37:5	74:11	112:0	149:5	186:11	224:0	261:5	298:11	336:0
3⅞	39:14	79:12	119:10	159:8	199:5	239:3	279:0	318:14	358:12
4	42:8	84:15	127:6	169:14	213:5	254:13	297:4	339:12	382:4
4⅛	45:3	90:5	135:8	180:11	225:14	271:0	316:4	361:7	406:10
4¼	48:0	95:15	143:14	191:13	239:12	287:11	335:10	383:9	431:9
4⅜	50:12	101:11	152:7	203:5	254:1	304:15	355:11	406:8	457:5
4½	53:12	107:8	161:5	215:0	268:12	322:11	376:5	430:2	483:13
4⅝	56:12	113:10	170:6	227:3	283:15	340:11	397:8	454:5	511:2
4¾	60:0	119:14	179:12	239:10	299:8	359:6	419:5	479:2	539:1
4⅞	63:2	126:3	189:5	252:6	315:8	378:10	441:11	504:12	567:13
5	66:12	133:8	200:5	267:0	333:12	400:8	467:5	534:0	600:12

EXPLANATION OF TABLES.

TABLE VII.—Continued.

Weight of Round Iron in Pounds and Ounces.

Size. Diameter in inches.	10 feet. lbs. oz.	11 feet. lbs. oz.	12 feet. lbs. oz.	13 feet. lbs. oz.	14 feet. lbs. oz.	15 feet. lbs. oz.	16 feet. lbs. oz.	17 feet. lbs. oz.	18 feet. lbs. oz.
½	6 : 11	7 : 5	8 : 0	8 : 11	9 : 5	10 : 0	10 : 11	11 : 5	11 : 14
⅝	10 : 7	11 : 8	12 : 8	13 : 9	14 : 10	15 : 10	16 : 11	17 : 12	18 : 13
¾	15 : 0	16 : 8	18 : 0	19 : 8	21 : 0	22 : 8	24 : 0	25 : 8	27 : 0
⅞	20 : 6	22 : 7	24 : 7	26 : 7	28 : 8	30 : 8	32 : 8	34 : 9	36 : 10
1	25 : 8	29 : 3	31 : 13	34 : 8	37 : 3	39 : 13	42 : 8	45 : 2	47 : 12
1⅛	33 : 9	37 : 0	40 : 5	43 : 11	47 : 0	50 : 6	53 : 12	57 : 2	60 : 8
1¼	41 : 11	45 : 14	50 : 1	54 : 4	58 : 6	62 : 9	66 : 12	70 : 14	75 : 1
1⅜	50 : 3	55 : 4	60 : 4	65 : 4	70 : 6	75 : 6	80 : 5	85 : 5	90 : 4
1½	59 : 11	65 : 11	71 : 10	77 : 10	83 : 9	89 : 9	95 : 10	101 : 8	107 : 8
1⅝	70 : 2	77 : 2	84 : 2	91 : 2	98 : 3	105 : 3	112 : 3	119 : 3	126 : 3
1¾	81 : 5	89 : 7	97 : 9	105 : 11	113 : 13	121 : 15	130 : 0	138 : 2	146 : 4
1⅞	93 : 5	102 : 11	112 : 0	121 : 5	130 : 11	140 : 0	149 : 5	158 : 11	168 : 0
2	106 : 2	116 : 12	127 : 6	138 : 0	148 : 10	159 : 4	169 : 14	180 : 8	192 : 2
2⅛	120 :	132 :	144 :	156 :	168 :	180 :	192 : 0	204 : 0	216 : 0
2¼	134 : 7	147 : 13	161 : 5	174 : 11	188 : 2	211 : 10	215 : 0	228 : 8	242 : 0
2⅜	149 : 12	164 : 12	179 : 12	194 : 11	209 : 11	224 : 11	239 : 10	254 : 10	269 : 10
2½	166 : 14	183 : 9	200 : 4	216 : 15	233 : 10	250 : 5	267 : 0	283 : 10	300 : 5
2⅝	187 : 8	206 : 4	225 : 0	243 : 12	262 : 8	281 : 4	299 : 11	318 : 12	337 : 8
2¾	200 : 12	220 : 13	240 : 15	261 : 1	281 : 1	301 : 2	321 : 3	341 : 5	361 : 6
2⅞	219 : 6	241 : 5	263 : 5	285 : 4	307 : 2	329 : 2	351 : 2	373 : 0	395 : 0
3	238 : 14	262 : 12	286 : 10	310 : 8	334 : 6	358 : 4	383 : 3	406 : 1	430 : 0
3⅛	259 : 5	285 : 4	311 : 3	337 : 1	363 : 0	388 : 14	414 : 12	440 : 11	466 : 10
3¼	280 : 7	308 : 7	336 : 8	364 : 8	392 : 9	320 : 10	448 : 10	476 : 11	504 : 11
3⅜	302 : 7	332 : 10	362 : 14	392 : 2	423 : 6	453 : 10	483 : 13	514 : 1	544 : 4
3½	325 : 2	357 : 10	390 : 2	422 : 10	455 : 3	487 : 10	520 : 3	552 : 12	585 : 5
3⅝	348 : 14	383 : 12	418 : 10	453 : 8	488 : 6	523 : 5	558 : 4	593 : 2	628 : 0
3¾	373 : 5	410 : 11	448 : 0	483 : 5	522 : 11	560 : 0	597 : 5	634 : 11	672 : 0
3⅞	398 : 10	438 : 8	478 : 6	518 : 4	558 : 2	598 : 0	637 : 13	677 : 11	717 : 9
4	424 : 10	467 : 2	509 : 9	552 : 1	594 : 8	637 : 0	676 : 6	621 : 14	764 : 6
4⅛	451 : 11	496 : 14	542 : 2	587 : 5	602 : 7	677 : 10	722 : 12	761 : 0	813 : 2
4¼	479 : 8	527 : 7	575 : 6	523 : 6	671 : 5	719 : 4	767 : 3	815 : 2	863 : 2
4⅜	508 : 3	559 : 0	609 : 13	660 : 10	711 : 6	762 : 4	813 : 0	863 : 15	914 : 11
4½	537 : 11	591 : 6	645 : 2	698 : 15	752 : 10	806 : 6	860 : 3	913 : 14	967 : 11
4⅝	567 : 15	624 : 11	681 : 8	738 : 3	795 : 0	851 : 13	908 : 10	965 : 6	1022 : 3
4¾	599 : 0	658 : 14	718 : 12	778 : 11	838 : 10	898 : 8	958 : 6	1018 : 5	1078 : 3
4⅞	630 : 15	694 : 0	757 : 2	820 : 3	883 : 5	946 : 6	1009 : 8	1072 : 10	1135 : 12
5	667 : 8	734 : 5	801 : 0	867 : 12	934 : 8	1001 : 5	1068 : 0	1134 : 12	1201 : 8

TABLE VIII.

This table exhibits at one view the weight and strength of various kinds of timber, as ascertained by actual experiments.

The estimates of the weight are made when the timber is well-seasoned and dry, but not kiln-dried.

There may appear to be a discrepancy between the strength of timber here given, and that found in the concluding remarks on Bridge Building; but it must be borne in mind that the calculations there made were on the greatest *safe* strain to which timber should be submitted for a long time without injury, or even impairing its elasticity, while the figures here given show the absolute strength, or the point of breakage.

TABLE VIII.
Weight and Strength of Timber.

Kind of Timber.	Weight compared with water—water being 1000.	No. of lbs. in a cubic foot.	No. of cubic feet in a ton.	Greatest tensile strength of a square inch in lbs.	Greatest safe strain upon a beam resting upon the ends, and loaded in the middle; per square inch in lbs.
White Oak, American	672	42	53	10200	800
English Oak	930	58	38	11800	875
Beech	850	42	45	12200	1000
Sycamore	600	38	59	9600	720
Chestnut	610	38	59	10650	650
Ash	845	52	43	14100	950
Elm	670	42	53	9700	700
Walnut	670	42	53	8800	675
Poplar	380	34	66	5900	380
Cedar	560	33	68	7400	400
White Spruce	550	34	66	10200	750
White Pine	590	37	60	12300	775
Yellow Pine	460	28	80	11800	770
Pitch Pine	660	41	54	9800	750
Fir	550	34	66	9500	675